Praise for *It's All About the Guest*

"Going to Davio's is an amazing experience. The attitude of the staff is always upbeat and attentive; the food is consistently superb. Steve has created a great business and has been able to replicate it in location after location with great training, motivation, and execution. This is the best business book that I have read since Tom Peters's *In Search of Excellence*. I believe that we are all in a service industry and this book is a must read—it's quick, easy, and funny. There are also a few great recipes!"

　　—Herb Chambers, one of America's largest automotive retailers

"During my Yankee years Davio's was my favorite place to go after the battles at Fenway. Win or lose! However, I must say the food seemed tastier after a victory. But on every occasion my party was always treated as if we were guests at Steve's home. Steve DiFillippo only knows how to treat people with respect. That's why *It's All About the Guest* is a must read, even if you are a Yankee fan."

　　—Joe Torre, MLB executive

"Steve is the consummate host. As restaurateurs both starting out in Boston in the late '80s, we share a passion for this industry as well as an enduring friendship. Through this book you will gain insight into what it takes to run a successful restaurant as Steve guides you through all aspects of the process, sharing stories from his own personal journey. It's all about bringing people around the table, and Steve always has room at his table to welcome you."

　　—Todd English, chef / restaurateur

"I have thoroughly enjoyed Steve's cooking during my career in Boston and had even greater pleasure getting to know Steve. Exceeding expectations is what he does best. I am sure people will enjoy this book as much as their experience at one of Steve's restaurants."

　　—Tom Brady, NFL quarterback

"Back in the early days of Aerosmith, Steve was just getting going with Davio's. It was one of the first high-end restaurants in Boston that paid respect to a younger clientele. It wasn't just the great food. It was the voice of a new place welcoming a generation on its way up. Steve's book is the journey of how he exceeded expectations to get to where he is today."

　　—Tom Hamilton, musician, Aerosmith

"This book may be all about the guest, but it is also all about the extraordinary attention to detail in every aspect of running a successful restaurant that Steve DiFillippo does so brilliantly in this very personal account of his journey of hard work from the bottom up to head of a restaurant empire that epitomizes his passionate love of food."

—*Mary Ann Esposito, host of* PBS Ciao Italia *and author of* Ciao Italia Family Classics

"Steve is an amazing restaurateur, and with *It's All About the Guest* he generously shares some of the secrets to his success. A fun read for anyone interested in the business, passionate about food, or just curious how life's lessons present themselves in some unexpected places."

—*Ming Tsai, chef / restaurateur*

"Steve DiFillippo is a world-class restaurateur. What sets him apart is that he treats every guest as if they were the only one in the restaurant. It's not just the best produce, meats, and fish. With Steve, the service is always equally important and the overall experience is all the better for it."

—*Jack Connors Jr., chairman emeritus, Hill, Holliday, Connors, Cosmopulos Inc.*

"I have many fond memories of Davio's on Newbury Street. It was a comfortable place to meet with friends, hang your hat, and knock a few back. Steve is not only a great restaurateur but an even better host. You will learn the business of hospitality from this book."

—*Peter Wolf, American rhythm and blues, soul, and rock and roll musician*

"From the incredible spring rolls (my favorite) to the outstanding service, there is much to be admired about Steve's successful business strategy. Whether you are a restaurant owner or aspiring entrepreneur, get your hands on this book and find out how Steve turned a dream into an empire."

—*Tedy Bruschi, former NFL linebacker*

"During my time with the Red Sox, I always enjoyed dining at Davio's Boston and getting to know Steve DiFillippo. *It's All About the Guest* is all about what makes Steve so successful in business and in life."

—*Kevin Youkilis, MLB player*

"Steve DiFillipo has the art of hospitality down to a science. Every nuance, every gesture of the experience of dining with Steve is pointed toward the same goal—to make the guest's experience extraordinary. Steve's restaurants are great places to celebrate (my wife and I met at Davio's and held our wedding reception there) and are, in themselves, cause for celebration!"

—*Keith Lockhart, conductor, Boston Pops Orchestra*

It's All About THE Guest

EXCEEDING EXPECTATIONS IN BUSINESS AND IN LIFE, THE DAVIO'S WAY

Steve DiFillippo

Foreword by Robert Kraft

LYONS PRESS
Guilford, Connecticut
An imprint of Globe Pequot Press

Lyons Press is an imprint of Globe Pequot Press.

Some names have been changed to protect the privacy of those involved.

Project Editors: Tracee Williams and Lauren Brancato
Text Design: Sheryl P. Kober
Layout: Mary Ballachino

Library of Congress Cataloging-in-Publication Data
DiFillippo, Steve.
It's all about the guest : exceeding expectations in business and in
life, the Davio's way / Steve DiFillippo.
    pages cm
 Summary: "When's the last time you picked up a business book that was
so engaging you couldn't put it down? Via entertaining stories from his
30-plus years as a top restaurateur, Steve DiFillippo illustrates essential
nuggets of wisdom—find your passion, pay attention, leave your ego
behind, keep your eye on the money, and more—advice that is applicable
in any business and in everyone's life"— Provided by publisher.
 ISBN 978-0-7627-9138-5 (hardback)
1. DiFillippo, Steve. 2. Restaurateurs—United States—Biography. 3.
Businessmen—United States—Biography. 4. Hospitality
industry—Management. I. Title.
 TX910.5.D495A3 2013
 647.95092—dc23
 [B]
                                                        2013019154

Printed in the United States of America

10 9 8 7 6 5 4 3 2 1

Mom and Dad. I'm so happy you met.
Thanks for your DNA.

Steve

Contents

Foreword

Steve DiFillippo is passionate about fine dining. He loves every part of the dining experience, from the creation of his recipes to the selection of ingredients to the preparation of the meal and the social engagement with friends and family at the dinner table. He studies food like our coaches study film. He is constantly looking for ways to improve his guests' experience, because Steve understands that in order to succeed in the restaurant industry, like so many other service industries, *it's all about the guest.*

I first met Steve in the mid-'80s, shortly after he bought his first restaurant. It was a small Italian place called Davio's, located on Newbury Street in Boston. He didn't know me at the time, but I remember how happy he seemed. He was a young, energetic, and charismatic restaurateur. You could tell that he genuinely loved what he was doing.

Prior to Steve's ownership, Davio's was a little-known, underperforming Italian restaurant competing in a saturated Boston marketplace. I am sure it was a huge financial risk for

Steve to buy the fledgling venue. But Steve saw an opportunity and seized it. He was bound and determined to pour his heart and soul into building the Davio's brand, making it one of Boston's premier fine-dining establishments.

I have always had an affinity for young entrepreneurs willing to take risks and accept the many challenges of ownership. In my businesses I have tried to deliver a quality product at reasonable prices, but where I gain my greatest advantage over the competition is in the customer service we provide. In my earliest observations of Steve, the interest of the guest was always paramount in his business plan, and in fact Steve earned my admiration and loyalty through his service. Of course, that is not to diminish Davio's food. It was—and still is—exceptional. It didn't matter what I ordered; every meal exceeded my expectations. From Steve's comfort foods to his daily specials, I often ended my meal proclaiming it the best I had ever had.

Thus was laid the foundation of a lasting relationship. Steve loved to create great meals. I loved to eat great meals. We became fast friends and have been ever since.

We have shared numerous dinners and holidays together. One of my favorite experiences was when Steve and his wife, Pam, accompanied me and my wife, Myra, to Israel on one of our annual missions in which we bring people from all religious backgrounds together to visit the Holy Land. I love exposing people to Israel—the birthplace of Judaism, Christianity, and Islam—and enjoy the reaction of my friends who visit for the first time. Guests on our missions are often overwhelmed by the confluence of spiritual and cultural histories juxtaposed with Israel's modern economy and culture. During the mission Steve was a sponge. He studied the region's history, asked poignant questions about the people's varied traditions, and immersed himself in the tasting and understanding of the cuisine. Steve said he was "blown away" by the experience and has since become an advocate and passionate defender of the country. Years later it was an honor to attend an Anti-Defamation League dinner in Boston at which Steve received the organization's Torch of Liberty award.

When my family decided to develop the property around Gillette Stadium with a retail and entertainment destination, Steve was the first restaurateur we called, and Davio's was the first restaurant to open at Patriot Place in 2008. Shortly after it opened, I took some guests who were in town for a Patriots game to Davio's for dinner. Despite owning and operating multiple restaurants, Steve was there to greet us and cater to our every want, just as he had when I first met him nearly thirty years before. The Patriots ended up winning that week and again later in the year when we repeated the dinner ritual. Superstitious as I am, Steve became our good luck charm. For years the Patriots were undefeated at home when Steve was able to attend one of our Friday night dinners.

In April 2011 Myra and I invited Steve to our home to attend a Seder dinner with our family. Steve brought his son Max. I will always remember the love and laughter shared that night as we celebrated the traditional meal, which would be Myra's last with us. Steve was always welcome, as our family adored his company, but more importantly, we appreciated his passion for learning about the Jewish culture and sharing in its traditions with our family.

When Steve told me he was writing this book, I couldn't wait to read it. *It's All About the Guest* is a tale of Steve's passionate pursuit of owning and operating a successful restaurant, a quest that began when he was a young boy growing up in Lynnfield, Massachusetts. It's a story of lessons learned along the way, and it provides a recipe for success for young entrepreneurs. As you would expect from Steve DiFillippo, it is very tastefully done and will be enjoyed by all.

Robert Kraft, Chairman and CEO, The Kraft Group
Owner, New England Patriots

Introduction:
A Question from My Wife

When I first told my wife, Pam, I wanted to write a book, she shot me a sarcastic look. "Why would *anybody* want to read a book by *you?*"

Good point, I thought. *Why would they?*

An answer came as I remembered an encounter I'd had while checking out pastas at Stop & Shop. A woman nearby said "hi!" enthusiastically, making it clear that she knew me from the restaurant. I'm familiar with hundreds, maybe thousands of our guests, but I couldn't remember when I had met her. Still, we must have had a friendly exchange because she was happy to see me and felt comfortable enough to ask a bunch of questions: How does Davio's make its Bolognese? What do you think about nonstick skillets? Do you really have to cook short ribs for hours? What's your opinion of food truck restaurants for young kids starting out? Her son, she told me, was waiting tables for the summer and wanted to open his own place someday. Would I mind meeting with him?

I told her I wouldn't mind, and that I also didn't mind handling her questions. I had long ago fallen in love with Bolognese, skillets, short ribs, and many other food topics. I got my first restaurant job when I was a sophomore studying business at Boston University. It was a three-hundred-seat place called Seaside, and I worked there for six years, starting as a coffee clerk and ending up as head chef, while also waiting tables the entire time. After graduation I got a degree from the Cambridge School of Culinary Arts while still working as a chef at Seaside. In 1985, when I was twenty-four years old, I bought my first restaurant, a small Italian place called Davio's on Boston's Newbury Street. It was about to go under, and in pretty short order I kicked out the druggies, redid the menu, lowered the prices, repealed the dress code, and turned the place around. Two years later, we'd tripled sales.

Today, I own seven restaurants, including Davio's in four states. In 2006 a serendipitous series of events led me to launch a line of Davio's frozen foods, which has become a big business that sells at three thousand stores in forty states— and counting. People come up to me asking about Davio's all the time—at cocktail parties, airports, my kids' sporting events. Friends and prominent guests call or text me at odd hours for recipe ideas, cooking tips, and other food-related or business advice.

Looking back on it, I was lucky to have an Italian grandmother and a Portuguese-American mother who were great cooks—and a father who was a successful businessman. On top of that, we had three restaurateurs as neighbors! I hung around those guys from the age of eleven and learned so much, especially from Mr. Sampsonas, who owned a restaurant I liked called The Continental. Both he and my father taught me something fundamental: It takes more to create a great restaurant than just a great chef and stellar food. *Restaurants are businesses, and they need to be run by businesspeople.*

Restaurants thrive because they're important places in peoples' lives. They offer guests a sense of community and comfort by giving them a nurturing experience they might not get anywhere else. I can boil the Davio's mission statement down to this: We want guests to have a great experience so they come back! Whenever I make a business decision, I ask myself the following question: *Will this make it better for our guests, or not?*

I also focus on a second set of guests, our team members. In order for the staff at any successful restaurant to deliver superior guest experiences, they have to treat each other well and be happy at work. Every entrepreneur knows that business is all about relationships. At Davio's we capture this concept in our notion of the *inner guest.* As restaurant workers we each are motivated to do our best when we're treated as nicely as we treat our paying guests. Treating each other well creates a positive, self-perpetuating cycle that fills seats and ultimately helps a restaurant to succeed.

It's All About the Guest explores the basics of running a restaurant as a successful business. It proceeds in a simple way, by telling stories. Back when I was a kid, I fired questions at Mr. Sampsonas the way so many people today fire them at me. His responses always stayed with me because they came peppered from top to bottom with cool, fun, interesting stories about stuff he'd lived through. Avoiding the dry and boring jargon of business books, the chapters that follow give an account of exactly how I've gotten where I always wanted to go and suggest how young chefs and aspiring restaurateurs can live their dreams, too.

I have always loved people and making money, so I have tried to learn everything I could about the industry I love. Hopefully this book will help would-be restaurateurs become aware of parts of the business they've never considered. That's not to say that you should read this book only if you're dreaming or thinking of opening a restaurant and want an insider's perspective. You should also read it if you're into food and want to know more about how a restaurant works. Or if you simply want to learn the ins and outs of what it takes to make money and build a sustainable business.

Pam, does this answer your question?

CHAPTER ONE

Passion

I've eaten a lot of sophisticated food in my time, but I still love a good hot dog. I'll never forget crossing paths with one of the richest, smokiest, plumpest, juiciest hot dogs of all time. It happened at a Seals & Crofts concert during the summer of 1974. I was thirteen years old and attending the concert with twenty other kids from Camp Kingsmont in western Massachusetts. Camp should be fun, but this wasn't a regular camp. It was a fat camp for what turned out to be pretty obese kids.

I wasn't obese—not by a long shot. The previous year, I had been captain of my Pop Warner football team, and the coach of the team really wanted me to come back. Unfortunately, I weighed 145, and the league had a firm weight limit of 120 pounds. So I went to my mom and told her I really wished I could play football again.

She thought it over. "Well, there's a camp out in the Berkshires. They'll help you lose weight."

"Mom . . . a fat camp?"

"Well, let's not call it a fat camp."

But it was a fat camp, and if I had known how un-fun it would be, I might not have gone. The first two weeks, I lost the desired twenty-five pounds and learned lots of great stuff about food—carbohydrates, proteins, vegetables, structured eating. It's amazing what happens when you don't have constant access to a refrigerator. But then I became bored with everything, the food included. When they offered us a chance to attend a series of concerts, I said yes. I didn't care so much about seeing Roberta Flack, John Denver, or James Taylor; I just wanted to get the heck out of camp.

It wasn't long before I caught sight of the hot dog stand. I would have bought a dog right then, but they were strictly off-limits. One of the counselors had made that perfectly clear a few nights earlier when we were driving home in the camp bus. In a stern voice he said, "Hey, so if anyone goes near those snack bars, your parents are going to be called tomorrow and you will be immediately sent home."

That did it. Don't ever tell me I can't do something. The way I looked at it, my weight was pretty normal. I had lost the pounds I had come to lose. There was no reason I couldn't have a hot dog. I just *had* to have one.

The week before our next concert, I plotted obsessively how I could get away from the group, buy a hot dog, and eat it without being seen. On the night of the concert, I wore a plain light blue T-shirt under the bright yellow Kingsmont shirts we all had to wear. In the middle of the show, while the band played "Diamond Girl" or "Summer Breeze," I walked off, went to the bathroom, and switched shirts in a private stall. Then I raced to the concession stand and bought a hot dog (with mustard). I made for the woods next to the concert shell to wolf it down. *Oh. My. God.* I hadn't eaten anything good for what felt like years. The camp was all cottage cheese and plain chicken breasts and salads with I don't know what for dressing, but nothing with any flavor.

Going crazy over a hot dog—or most any other kind of super-delicious food—was typical for me as a kid. When I was nine the spread at my cousin Mona's wedding at Boston's Copley Plaza Hotel *blew . . . my . . . mind.* There was a huge raw bar with shrimp, oysters, and clams. This was more than forty years ago, before you saw things like that. I ate at least five lobster tails and told my mother it was the greatest day of my life. When I was sixteen a caterer named Roberta Dowling got my attention. My sister Donna was getting married, and Roberta converted our house and property into what looked and functioned like a gorgeous restaurant. We again had a huge raw bar, fine linens, filet mignon—unbelievable. I was wildly inspired; I told Roberta, "I'm going to have my own restaurant, just you watch." She didn't believe me, but as luck would have it, I later studied under her at the school she owned, the Cambridge School of Culinary Arts. How cool is that?

Throughout my childhood I thought about every plate that came my way—every lunch, every dinner, every snack. At my friends' houses I paid close attention to what they had in their kitchens and what their parents served for dinner. In high school I was the only guy who took home economics, just so I could learn about cooking. From a very young age, I saw eating as this exciting activity that everybody got to do every day *that felt so good.* I didn't yet recognize the power of food to bring people together, express love, or ground us in the world. I just thought how great it was to eat. I loved smelling food,

3

touching it, tasting it, feeling it on my tongue, swallowing it. It was pure pleasure.

It's not normal to be so obsessed with food, but that's what you have to have to be in this business—*obsessed.* It's too difficult in too many ways to own a restaurant unless you possess a deep, undying passion for eating and feeding people. What's hard about it? The hours, for one thing. They're long, they're nights, and they include weekends and holidays. Forget about regular dinners at home. Forget about being there for Mother's Day, Thanksgiving, Valentine's Day, Christmas Eve. Those are busy, busy days. Working when most of the rest of the world is off at home is hard. And as hard as it is on you, it's harder on your family. Because even though you don't really want to work at night—you *kind of do,* and your family knows this.

Being passionate about something is like having a mistress you're always half wanting to take off and be with, which hurts the people closest to you (not that I've had a mistress myself; I'm just speculating). A lot of passionate people—driven people—are hard to live with, and their families take the hit. Many of my restaurant friends have gotten divorced, including me. You have to find a strong significant other who understands the nature of the business. I didn't get it right the first time, but luckily, I did the second.

Unless you love food and serving people, you're not going to want to make the constant sacrifices, and if you don't, you will not succeed at this business. It's passion that sustains you through the long hours, the snowstorms, the recessions, the fear that you can't make it, and if you have made it, the fear that you'll lose it. I'm always advising people to find their passion, because despite all the hardships of this business, I don't think of what I do every day as work; I think of it as fun. And if you're really lucky, you'll feel passionate about business as well as eating, because the numbers have to add up or you can't serve the food you love.

Look at restaurants that have made it over a long period, and you'll find that their owners are almost always men and women who think about food, eating, and business an unnatural amount of time. On the flip side, so many places go out of business because their owners don't have their hearts and souls in it. I see it over and over again. I have to laugh when I hear that somebody wants to open a restaurant when they retire—as though it's an easy thing to do when you don't really have to work anymore. You can't open a restaurant because you want to have a place where your friends can have drinks and dinner. Ever wonder what the story is behind those places that close before it seems they've even opened? Now you know.

If you're thinking of starting a restaurant, you need to sit down and ask yourself: "Do I really have what it takes to succeed? Do I love food and making money enough to make these things my life?"

꙳

In answering these questions, keep in mind that a passion for eating, food, and business can't be manufactured. It has to be in your blood. It has to run deep. Food was a central part of the culture I grew up in. My mother, the pretty, red-haired daughter of Portuguese immigrants who had emigrated from the Azores to Providence, Rhode Island, was the cook. When she married into my father's Italian family, she was allowed—and expected—to learn all the DiFillippo family recipes from her mother-in-law. This, however, was permitted only after the knot had been officially tied. You'd think these recipes were state secrets! In a way, they were. My Italian grandparents also weren't born in this country. Only one of them spoke English well enough to be understood. Of course the familiar foods of their childhoods would give them a sense of emotional security.

For me, too, food accounts for many warm, comforting memories. Throughout my childhood we spent most Sundays and holidays eating at relatives' houses all day. This was heaven for me. Both my mother's and father's families lived in Providence, where my parents grew up and met. Most weeks, we'd take an hour-and-a-half-long drive from our house in Lynnfield, Massachusetts, to Providence and make the rounds, eating everywhere we went.

We started at my Aunt Angie and Uncle Tony's home. It's a good family laugh to this day that my mother and her sister Angie—nice Portuguese-American girls—both married Italian-American guys named Tony. Angie loved to cook, and Uncle Tony had a big garden, a *huge* garden, and grew everything. He was into canning things, too. His basement was like a grocery store, he had so much put up—shelves of peppers and tomatoes, green beans, and beets. I used to drive Tony crazy with my questions: How does canning work? How long do different plants take to grow? How come the soil doesn't get old when you use it year after year in your garden? It was thanks to Uncle Tony that I first learned what a fresh vegetable really was. This was before Whole Foods, and before we brought in fresh fruits and vegetables all year long from places like Mexico or Chile. You couldn't get very much high-quality, fresh produce in the supermarket.

My Aunt Angie was a great cook, and she made both Italian and Portuguese dishes. We never had Portuguese specialties like kale soup and seafood stews at home unless my father was away, since he doesn't like them. Angie's Italian dishes weren't the same as my mother's and grandmother's, though. She made her meatballs with breadcrumbs, whereas my mother made hers with stale bread soaked in milk, which made them moister and softer. When I first opened Davio's and changed the menu, I got rid of the typical Italian-American dishes, including meatballs. But about five years ago, I put meatballs back on our menu. Happy I did, because they're just so good!

I didn't appreciate Angie's cooking so much then, as I had picked up a bit of my father's cautiousness around food. Still, I always ate at least some of everything, and I especially liked Angie's clams and her baked goods—she made great pies and cinnamon twists. I also loved her pesto. Uncle Tony grew bushels of basil, and during the summer my mother spent two days with her sister making tons of pesto that they froze. Aunt Angie herself hated pesto—she made it just for our family, which said a lot about the kind of person she was. Years later, when I worked as a chef at Seaside, I made gallons of it as well in the summer and froze it for wintertime use at the restaurant. In those days, the early '80s, you couldn't get fresh basil during the winter, and I wanted to serve pesto year-round.

Don't tell anybody in the DiFillippo family, but here's Aunt Angie's pesto recipe.

Aunt Angie's Basil Pesto

In summer when herbs are freshest, take **2 cups basil, ½ cup extra virgin olive oil** (Monini preferred), **2 tablespoons pine nuts, 1 small clove garlic, ½ cup fresh parsley,** and a **pinch of salt,** and blend it all together in a food processor. Put this mixture in a jar and freeze it. Then in January, when it's freezing cold and snowing outside, take out the jar and defrost it on the counter for a couple of hours. Put the contents in a small stainless steel bowl, add **2 tablespoons butter, 2 tablespoons grated Parmigiano cheese, 2 tablespoons grated Romano cheese,** and **salt and pepper** to taste. Mix the pesto with some freshly cooked pasta. (A little trick: If you want your pesto to have the consistency of a sauce, add in **2 ounces of cooking water** from the pasta.) And there you go—fresh pesto. It's like eating out of your garden in the middle of winter. There's nothing better!

After visiting Aunt Angie and Uncle Tony, we usually headed across Providence to my father's parents' triple-decker on Pomona Avenue and ate again there. Of my grandparents, only my father's mother, whom I called Nana, spoke conversational English. I loved climbing the stairs to her house because there was always something cooking on the stove in a small, black cast iron skillet. Glancing behind me, I'd steal a piece—and then another. I can still taste the deep flavor of her meats. She used that skillet when she taught Aunt Marie, my mother, and me how to cook. I still adore my grandmother's marinara, meatballs, eggplant, and chicken Parmesan—classic Italian-American dishes I'd learned to make by the age of twelve.

More than the dishes themselves, I learned from Nana that food mattered and how you prepared it mattered. Shopping in a grocery store? Unthinkable! She bought all of her raw materials from small, specialty vendors in Federal Hill, Providence's Italian neighborhood. What does the meat guy know about fish? What does the fish guy know about vegetables? That was her attitude. She wanted the best of everything to go into her dishes. And cook she did—all day long, in small batches (necessary, she explained, to make sure that every part of a dish is evenly done). Often she would come stay with us and cook with my mom, peeling garlic, cutting eggplant, and standing over my mom's shoulder, watching her every move, making sure she executed perfectly the DiFillippo family recipes to which she'd been given access. Looking back on it, I think Nana might have left a key ingredient or two out of each recipe when she gave them to my mother; somehow the same dishes always tasted just a little bit better when Nana made them herself at her house.

A couple months after Nana died, in the early '90s (on my birthday, as it happened), my father invited us to come down and take whatever we wanted of her things. My relatives took useful items, like TVs, chairs, and tables. I had a successful restaurant by then and was after only one thing. I walked into the kitchen and saw that black cast iron pan sitting there on my grandmother's 1940s white stove—the only time I ever saw it empty. Grabbing it, I walked down the old squeaking staircase and went to my car. My father was out on the lawn. "Why aren't you taking anything?" he asked.

I held up the skillet. "I have everything I want." He looked at me like I was crazy, so I decided to explain myself. "This started it all for me, Dad. I'm not sure where I'd be today if it wasn't for Nana."

He looked at me, my father, and it was the only time I ever saw tears in his eyes. To this day, I keep that pan out in my home kitchen, on a shelf above the stove. I cook with it often.

~

Our final stop on Sundays was to visit Aunt Marie and Uncle Aldo, who lived in a beautiful house in Weston, Massachusetts, outside Boston. By the time we got there each week, it was 6:00 or 7:00 p.m., and they had already eaten. We had been eating all day, but in my family, we couldn't visit together and not eat. Eating is just what we did—and still do. At Marie and Aldo's, we sat around the living room talking for ten or fifteen minutes and then, inevitably, Aldo got up and went into the kitchen. I followed him, along with my mother and grandmother, while Aunt Marie and my father sat on the couch talking with everyone else.

I loved watching Aldo lay out the food. I thought it was the coolest thing that he was an extremely successful businessman who also loved being in the kitchen. My father was a businessman—president of the company Aldo had founded—yet he never cooked, and still doesn't. Aldo showed me that it was okay for men to love to cook and serve. Remember, this was the late '60s and early '70s, before chefs became widely visible and admired.

Grounded in the southern Italian region of Calabria, Aldo's food was different from my Nana, who was from Naples. Along with good leftovers, Aldo would put out some cold cuts, including sharp provolone cheese, which we didn't have at home. He also served anchovies and sautéed calamari with olive oil and lemon—foods I'd never had anywhere else. Nobody made calamari back then. In fact, thanks to Aldo, I became one of the first chefs to offer calamari as a special at Seaside during the early '80s. I remember that a veteran waiter named Rob Mahoney asked me what it was when I put it out the first time. He didn't have a clue. When I told him it was a kind of seafood, he said, "Oh, really, seafood? I just told people out there it was luncheon meat." I'm not making that up.

On visits to Marie and Aldo's, we ate together at their great big dining room table. Marie and Aldo's oldest daughter, whose wedding feast I had flipped over when I was nine, had married a very liberal guy, a professor at a Canadian university. My father and Aldo were more conservative, especially Aldo, who plastered his sliding glass doors with Nixon stickers so no one mistakenly walked into them. Thinking back on it, those stickers must have killed my cousin's husband, Harvey. But Aldo stood his ground. He loved Nixon and never stopped defending him.

Imagine me sitting there at Aldo's table, a kid eating as much pepperoni, provolone, and mortadella as he wanted while listening to the grown-ups argue political subjects. I was fascinated by these conversations and learned a lot; everything everybody said sounded so knowledgeable, interesting, and right. I realize now how special it was that these discussions didn't turn into angry arguments—that members of our family could disagree so profoundly yet remain good humored. I learned then never to use my position at my restaurants to prove a point or win an argument. I also learned that food had this special power to bring people together, to help them relax, come alive, and live in the moment. The whole point of food is not merely to nourish the body, but to nourish us as people, as the social beings we are.

To do well in restaurants, you have to love socializing just as much as food, eating, and business. One of the best feelings in the world to me today is working in one of my restaurants when all the tables are full and 250 people are eating our food, laughing, and talking up a storm. It's the same happiness I knew sitting over food with my family back in the day, the same fulfillment I sought when I raced around the kitchen as a kid making something for my brother and sister, mother, or father to eat.

Being the person who structures or enables social life each and every day is sometimes hard. Running a restaurant is like holding a constant open house or party. Even if you're a natural extrovert, it takes effort to remain responsive to the many moods of your guests as they come in the door. It can be 7:00 p.m., on a day when you started work at 10:00 a.m., and a party comes in wanting to do shots with you. And of course you can't: You're *working*. It takes effort and skill to avoid killing their buzz while gently extricating yourself from their party. Then you might turn to greet another guest who's in a bad mood, ready to get totally annoyed over nothing. He's miserable and thinks it's your job to make him happy. There are indifferent guests, too, and so many wonderful, easygoing guests—and you don't want to neglect them while responding to your more demanding guests.

Then there are those who want to ask your advice about a million different things right in the middle of service. Restaurateurs are highly visible and accessible, so people think to ask them for their opinions on lots of topics simply because we're *there*. I've built so many restaurants and had years of experience with contractors, designers, suppliers, repair people—you name it. Meanwhile, I'm a landlord, employer, manager—and a father, too. People know all this, so they ask me where my kids go to school, the name of a great tile guy, or how to find a good commercial real estate agent.

A great restaurateur has to be able to maintain his or her poise and react hospitably to every guest, *because success absolutely depends on good guest experiences*—which is, after all, why most of us got into the business! This takes social agility, grace, and some serious physical and emotional fortitude. It's something you can't do well, over and over again for years, unless you really do love interacting with people. After growing up in a warm and boisterous Italian and Portuguese family, with so many distinct personalities and strong opinions, I had little doubt that I did.

When you're passionate about something, and when you act on that passion, you naturally and effortlessly learn what you need to learn in order to succeed. When I was twenty-three, the year before I bought Davio's, I went to Europe with my girlfriend and my good friend Charlie, who was a great eater. All I wanted to do was go to restaurants and see what and how they cooked. We had a three-week Eurail pass and ate our way through London, Paris, Nice, Monte Carlo, Barcelona, Rome, and Venice. I gained about fifteen pounds. At the time, the exchange rate was great for Americans, which made it cheap to eat out.

One night, after a great five-course dinner in Venice, we walked out of the restaurant and I said, "Charlie, why don't we—"

He cut me off. "Yeah, let's go to another restaurant."

And we did. When we finished that second meal, we went back to the first place for a drink. We liked the little restaurant, and the chef-owner had been friendly to us. It had a tiny dining room, maybe thirty-five seats around wooden tables, everything all mismatched and make-do. The place had emptied out by then, and we told the owner what we'd just done: eaten a second dinner. He loved that we cared about food so much. I had just graduated culinary school and was working as a chef full time; I wanted to learn everything I could about restaurants.

The owner spoke some English, and we drank amaretto (which I couldn't stand, but what the hell) and espresso and talked about food until 2:00 a.m. Naturally, I got myself into his kitchen. I'd been inside a lot of restaurant kitchens by that time. As a kid I had gone on business trips to other cities with my father, and I would always go snooping around hotel kitchens. By fifteen, when I was earning some decent part-time money, I went to as many restaurants as I could and either talked my way into the kitchen or spied on it somehow. That same year, I impersonated my older brother at the DMV and got myself a fake driver's license so I could take my parents' car and drive into Boston to go to restaurants. Although I was an otherwise good kid, I didn't think twice about doing this; I was not to be denied when it came to food and restaurants.

Anyhow, in this little kitchen in Venice, I saw them cooking pasta to order by keeping a large pot of water boiling all day, and then taking smaller pots from the mother pot to cook individual orders. I thought it was amazing! Thanks to my grandmother, I always knew and loved good pasta. She'd taught my mother to cook it al dente, like she did. (My childhood friend Brian O'Hearn would always ask what was wrong with my mother's pasta—it was so hard. Yeah, but he loved it!) But I didn't know how to cook pasta on demand, order after order. When I opened Davio's, we borrowed this little trick from the Venetians, using an enormous, fifty-gallon pot for the mother pot. Today, we have very expensive stainless steel machines that hold that much boiling water and automatically self-fill. But even before we had such high-tech equipment, we never dunked precooked pasta. No way. And that was pretty unusual in 1985.

Another, even more basic revelation about food that flowed from my passion occurred when I was twelve. My sister was nearly five years older than me, my brother four, so my parents had started to go away on weekends and leave us kids alone. My mother would lay out food for us in the refrigerator and freezer, and I always ended up being the one to take it out and make something for us. My sister, Donna, was supposed to be the responsible one, but really, I was more responsible. This was, after all, the early '70s, and she was a teenager with her parents away. Food was the last thing on her mind, boys the first. I was just a kid who loved food and cooking and serving people, so I did it.

One weekend when our parents were away, I took a package of chicken out of the freezer and set it out to defrost. A few hours later, when I removed the butcher's paper, I found that there was no chicken in the chicken, just bones. I flipped out!

Not only was I starving to death and frustrated that there wasn't any meat, but I also feared that my mother might be going crazy. Around this same time, she had begun acting oddly. She'd always been the nicest mother, but now she had become kind of mean sometimes and moody. She was also always hot, always talking about the temperature, about how great it was if a little breeze kicked up. In the middle of winter, we'd be cold, and she'd be opening up the sliding glass doors and complaining about the heat. Now here she was, freezing garbage instead of throwing it away.

I put the bones in the refrigerator so I could confront her with them when she got home. The next day, I did exactly that. "Mom, I have to talk to you. What's going on? You've been acting weird lately, and I don't understand it. And yesterday, I take the chicken out of the freezer, and all that's in there is bones and nothing to make. Are you going crazy?"

My mother broke out laughing. "Oh, you think I'm losing my mind?"

"You are!" I said, defiant and fed up. "You're hot all the time, you're moody, and now you're freezing garbage!"

"Well," she said, smiling and fanning herself. "I promise you, Stevie, I'm not crazy. I freeze bones all the time. Let me show you what I do with them."

As I looked on, she put the bones in a big roasting pan and into the oven to brown for about an hour. She then got a couple of carrots, onions, and celery stalks and threw them in the same roasting pan, roasting it all together for about another twenty minutes. She took everything in the roasting pan, put it in a big pot, and covered it with water, white wine, and a *bouquet garni*. "I'm making chicken stock," she told me.

She explained that a stock was like water flavored with vegetables, spices, bones, and leftover meat. "I use stocks as a base for lots of things, but mostly for the kale soup you love so much."

Now, I'd been helping my grandmother and mother cook for a couple years, but this stock, this was different. Until then, everything I'd ever cooked or seen cooked was made to be eaten just as it was. But we weren't going to eat this stock; we were going to use it to make other dishes, like soups and sauces. I couldn't believe it. It had never even entered my mind that cooks made things to then make into other things. Like that, a whole new level of complexity and even mystery around cooking opened up for me. I loved it more than ever.

After the stock was finished, the house smelled beautiful—like my mother's kale soup. It was an earthy, multilayered, deeply soothing aroma. It turned me on in a way I hadn't experienced before, have never forgotten, and still love. I love it every day when I walk into one of our restaurants and Jaime or Antonio or one of our other morning prep cooks has several enormous vats of stock at the simmer. Davio's is very big on stock: We make chicken, veal, lobster, and fish stocks daily. If we're serving a lamb special that day, we make lamb stock. Stocks are the basis of all our sauces, risottos, and soups and many of our pasta dishes.

I still love to dip a spoon into a fifty-quart pot of stock and pull out a small, tender piece of chicken or snag a veal bone and suck on it.

So good.

I've had dozens, hundreds, of small epiphanies that today inform everything that we do at Davio's. And yes, I'm still crazy about food. When I open my eyes in the morning, my first thoughts usually concern what I'm going to eat that day. I get a rush at 7:00 a.m. remembering that the chefs are doing a homemade ravioli dish for a special event that night, or that Nantucket scallops are in. I might lie there for a minute fantasizing about the sound those scallops make when they hit the skillet. I also continue to repeat the multiple-meal motif of my childhood Sundays. When I travel to another city, I almost always make three reservations. I start around 5:00 p.m., having an appetizer somewhere and checking out the food and the operation. After the first place I head to a 7:30 p.m. dinner reservation somewhere else, and I hit my final destination—again for dinner as well as drinks and dessert—around 10:00 p.m.

Being at my own restaurants never gets old. Mid- to late afternoons is when it really hits—the itchiness I feel to get to one of our locations if I'm not there already. I love the time just before dinner when everything is pure potential. The kitchen has prepped all day, the servers are ready, and the place looks beautiful. Outside on the street, people are getting off work. Who knows what the night will bring? Will we be busy? Who's going to come in? Will we run into any problems? Will we hit it out of the park? An hour and a half later, the place is packed, everyone's working at capacity, and the thousands of details that have been set in place mesh and come alive, bringing the restaurant into its fullest expression. It's like riding a twenty-foot wave or a bucking bronco. Thrilling beyond belief. Just incredible.

If you're lucky enough to be living your passion, no matter what your business, I congratulate you. And if you're not yet doing so, what are you waiting for? Start working at it—you'll never be bored or unhappy. When I was twenty, my dad expected that I'd join our large and very successful family company. It was a great financial opportunity and hard to pass up, but ultimately I had to follow my dreams. Over the years, I will admit that despite my love of food I sometimes doubted whether I'd made the right choice, especially when I saw how successful my brother, Dave, was working with my dad. Today, having survived both good times and bad, I'm happy with my decision. I'm also proud to see my daughter Katherine following in my footsteps and pursuing her own passion as a social worker, even though she could have a comfortable career at Davio's.

When I think back on that hot dog I enjoyed so many years ago, I realize that much of the thrill was actually the fun of the hot-dog stand, the mystery of what that little stand might serve. Even today, when I can eat nearly anything I want anytime, I am still thrilled to find a clam shack, say, at a strange ferry terminal or a pizza place that's new to me. As I've explained, it's not just the food I'm attracted to, but everything—the whole experience around eating. We build temples for this experience—they're called restaurants—and I love them.

Always have. Always will.

Restaurant Lessons to Live By

If you don't have a passion for eating and feeding people, don't bother trying to become a restaurateur. You'll never make it.

You can feel pretty certain a career path is for you if you think of the long hours as fun, not work.

To succeed as a restaurateur, it's not enough to love food. You also have to love business and being around people.

Your passion for the restaurant business can't be skin deep. It has to go to the core of your personality and childhood experiences.

If you really do have a passion for something, then don't waste time. Get cracking—everything else you need will fall into place.

CHAPTER TWO

Set the Tone

When I first took over Davio's on May 6, 1985, the place was hanging by a thread. I mean a *thread*. Almost nothing was working right at this eighty-seat Italian restaurant. The name, Davio's, was a mistranslation of the Italian for "David" (it's supposed to be "Davide") made by the original owner. Maybe I should have taken that as a sign and backed off, but I was out of my mind crazy to own my own restaurant. And good thing, too, because it was going to take everything I had to turn the place around.

The task was daunting. I had to fix what I could and set a new course in a dozen different ways as fast as possible *without disrupting operations,* such as they were. I'd purchased the place from a team of remote owners who had been doing little more than stopping by once in a while to take cash from the safe. Nobody had been managing the business, and the operation was in free fall: There were no schedules posted, drugs and alcohol were rampant in the kitchen, the food was subpar, the place was dirty, morale was nonexistent, and service was abysmal. The staff was narcissistically partying their way through work as though they were starring in a sitcom where the guests were mere extras. But to me, restaurants were *all about the guest*—so you can imagine how many changes I had to make.

Prior to buying the place, I'd worked it for two weeks under the guise of being the new general manager. As a result, I knew where all the bodies were buried. But I also knew the potential. Despite the many problems Davio's had, it still enjoyed a good name. The restaurant had opened six years earlier, and it had been very successful for several years. Restaurants can take a few years to lose their reputation, and Davio's at the time was right at the edge. Meanwhile, Davio's had much that I wanted: It was a good, manageable size; the lease was fantastic; and the restaurant was located on Boston's trendiest street. Also, it had an underutilized second floor bar and outdoor patio, both of which had phenomenal commercial potential. The owners had been grossing only about $700,000 a year; Seaside, where I'd worked as a chef, was doing $5 million, so I had a decent idea of what Davio's was capable of and what I had to do to scale up operations.

Although I was only twenty-four, I knew that if I didn't grab the reins right away and set a totally new tone for the operation, there wouldn't be a Davio's in six months. I had to assume control. I had to lead this little crew to create the kind of restaurant *I* wanted. Any owner must be able to lead, so if you're looking to start a restaurant or any other business, you might want to ask yourself if you have the personality for it. I can't say I was the smartest kid growing up, but I was always the leader. I was the one who took over, assumed responsibility, spoke up, and organized whatever group I was part of. Taking control at Davio's was natural for me.

The people we had on staff certainly called out for leadership. We had all kinds of problems—mice problems, price problems, equipment problems, vendor problems, money problems—but the source of them all was staff problems. Not only was almost everyone drinking or high, but they weren't even hiding it. The chefs were doing cocaine on the line openly (remember, this was the '80s). Servers were racing in and out of the bathroom still snorting coke into noses dusted with telltale white powder. Almost no one on the staff cared a thing about the restaurant, the guests, or anything beyond making as much money as fast as possible so they could go out and *really* party.

Jose, the dishwasher, was doing more business out the back door than what was coming in the front. I'd keep hearing knocks on the kitchen door and watch Jose leave and come back. It took me about five knocks to get it. The chef, Sammy, a very talented guy from New York City, had a substance abuse problem a lot worse than the out-of-control recreational use of the average team member. He'd work for a stretch then disappear for three days; you never knew if he was going to show up.

At the first staff meeting—which in itself was a new thing for this group—I announced that rules were coming down the pike. I would no longer tolerate drug and alcohol use during work, and I would fire anybody caught using. I wound up canning seven team members for snorting up that first year. But drugs weren't responsible for all of Davio's staff problems. The front-of-house guy was unstable—tragically so, as it would turn out. Alex Reynolds, the face of Davio's, was an extremely good-looking, model-type guy in his early thirties. He had a girlfriend at the time, and they were always breaking up, making up, or fighting. Before I took over he spent more time on the phone with her than actually running the place. He would leave the podium unattended on a busy Saturday night and wander back in eating ice cream forty minutes later.

And then there was Oscar Rowe, Alex's partner and right-hand man. These two guys each still owned small parts of the restaurant—2 and 3 percent, respectively. Rowe was a wine connoisseur and the closest thing Davio's had to a manager. But—big but—he was a born-again Christian obsessed with getting people to join the Church of Christ. He'd meander around the restaurant with a Bible and ask you to open to any page. "Point your finger at a paragraph," he'd say. Then he'd explain at length why the passage you selected applied perfectly to your current circumstances. This might have been helpful in some other situation, but I needed revenue more urgently than a prayer. Our vendors had lost all faith in the previous owners and would only supply us on a cash-on-delivery basis. Davio's owed everybody: the meat guy, the fish guy, the liquor guy, even the IRS. Oscar's shtick wasn't getting the job done.

My first move was to fix our kitchen, starting with the salad refrigerator. A week earlier, I'd been served a salad at Davio's that had been insanely wilted. When I'd asked one of the so-called managers what was up with the salad, he told me that the prep fridge was broken and there was no money to get it fixed.

"Are you nuts?" I said. "You're going to kill somebody! You can't be using a salad station if it doesn't function."

The air temperature inside the fridge was warmer than ambient air. So I called the restaurant's refrigeration guy and wrote him a check. Right after that, though, I switched to the refrigerator guy I'd used at Seaside, Gary Bennett. I eventually did the same with almost all my service people and food vendors—switched over to guys whom I trusted and who trusted me. Many of them I still use. I also visited Davio's existing vendors, introduced myself, and got to know them. As soon as I did that in those first weeks, the quality of our produce and other foods got much better. Establishing trust and a personal relationship is fundamental to all business relationships.

The refrigerator taken care of, I concentrated on our kitchen staff. Within a few days of my takeover, Sammy the chef pulled one of his disappearing acts and didn't come in, so I fired him. I'll never forget calling my dad up and telling him. "Hey, Dad," I said. "I fired the chef today."

He thought I'd lost my mind. "Oh my God, Jennie, he fired the chef!" he said to my mother, in the background.

"But, Dad, the guy was completely unreliable, and I can't have that. Don't worry. I'm a chef; I'll take over."

And I did—for the first month or two. But even though I loved cooking, I didn't want to be confined to the kitchen. I knew I could contribute the most, create the best restaurant, by also working the front of the house. It's essential for owners to know their strengths, use them to their fullest, and get stellar talent in other areas. So I called a couple great cooks I knew from my culinary school, Bob Buoniconti and Ralph Bryant, and made Bob the head chef. I trusted these guys; I knew they'd show up clean and sober and get the job done. I'd also inherited two very good, very fast cooks when I bought Davio's—Scottie and Paulie. Thank God for them.

So, really, the kitchen was in decent shape early on, even though not a single recipe had been written down. But that hardly mattered because my plan was to entirely revamp the menu as soon as I got the more acute problems under control.

The second week, I began retooling our front of house by firing the best server, a French guy called François. He was an unbelievably skilled seller and server—he could take the whole floor. Unfortunately, he treated his colleagues poorly. Instead of helping a fellow server through a busy moment by getting a new table a drink order or bread, he'd grab the table. And losing a table costs a server a significant tip. François could have helped his coworkers instead of stealing their tables, but he wasn't a team player. We wanted team players at the new Davio's.

Firing François showed the other staff that I was serious about the professionalism I wanted our staff to have. I knew I had to set a tone and establish the culture I wanted. Firing someone is never fun, but when it's necessary, you have to be able to do it—and move on.

I had a talk with another server about his arrogance. Tonino, a handsome, dark-haired Italian, is today the most requested server at Davio's and one of my most trusted team members and friends. Back then, he still had some growing up to do. When people ordered something he didn't approve of, like a salad for dinner, he gave attitude, crunching up his face and making a disapproving expression with his lips.

I brought him outside by the dumpster one evening and said, "Okay. The chef's gone. François is gone. Are you going to be next? Because I don't want you to treat guests like they're privileged to be at your table. That's not the attitude we want in this restaurant. So, please, either get behind the way I want guests treated or go someplace else." Tonino didn't say much that night, but he saw that we were going to change things at Davio's, and he wanted to be a part of it.

Today, at our restaurants hardly anybody ever gets fired. We say you have to fire yourself at Davio's, and that's exactly what happens: The culture is so strong that people get the message and leave on their own when the fit isn't right. But back then, I had to set a course.

＝

In those early weeks I sat at one of the tables in the late afternoons, after the lunch rush, thinking of new ways to bring in money. One day, I was sitting at Table 43 with my yellow pad, worrying away, when Oscar Rowe sat down next to me and opened his Bible. "Steve, here, read this passage. It will help you get through this." I looked down at the book, and it said, "Do not worry."

Somehow, the sight of that passage made me snap. I shut his Bible and gave it back to him. "You know, Oscar," I said, "I need more than the Bible right now. I need some help and some money. So, thank you very much, but see you later." I got up from the table, went over to the phone, and called my longtime lawyer, Jim Rudolph. When I bought Davio's, I had agreed to keep Oscar on for two months so he'd have time to find another job. I told Jim to call Rowe's lawyer and get him out of Davio's that week. And he did. We paid Oscar off. It was a financial strain, but this clown was making it impossible to implement the professional atmosphere I had to establish.

Alex Reynolds was a different story.

A few weeks after I took over, Alex went to Florida to see his girlfriend. They'd split, and he wanted to patch things up. When he got there he found her living with another guy. He went back to his hotel, climbed up to the roof, and jumped. Dead.

It was absolutely tragic. I felt terrible about it. I was acquainted with Alex from all the times I'd eaten at Davio's in the year before I bought the place, and I felt sad. I also felt even more under siege. There I was, twenty-four years old, and the face of Davio's kills himself three weeks after I take over.

＝

On the plus side, two of Davio's front-of-house guys turned out to be valuable assets. Jeff Gates, a server before I took over, ended up managing. He became a close friend and still is. Fifteen months after taking over Davio's, when I finally allowed myself three weeks off to get married, I was able to do it because I knew Jeff could handle everything.

Jeff was very detail-oriented, and he and I started to keep extensive notes on guests in our big reservation book at the podium up front. We jotted down names, hair colors, and wives' or girlfriends' names (or both). We jotted down whether guests preferred booths; if they were slow eaters (so we'd know how to schedule reservations after them); what their favorite cocktails and wines were. We also noted negatives—that they didn't like particular servers, or that we'd overcooked their meat on previous visits. I'd realized early on that regular guests loved to be known. So when a guest walked in, I said, "Oh, Mr. Appel, we have your booth all ready for you," and he sat down and his cocktails or favorite appetizer arrived minutes later. Today, we have all the client information we can gather in our computer, but back then it was all handwritten in our reservation book.

The other great team member I inherited was the bartender, Tommy Forti Jr. He was twenty-three years old, great looking, and smart. He read all the time and knew all the sports stats. If a Red Sox player got traded at 3:00 p.m., Tommy immediately knew why management had made the change and could reel off the guy's batting average and career history. Remember, this was before the Internet. Tommy was popular with everybody. Guys loved to talk to him about sports, and women just loved him, period.

Within the first six months, a few former colleagues from Seaside started waiting tables at Davio's. I would never poach team members from another place, but these guys, my friends, wanted a change and they found me. Howard Quinby III and Alan Krivitsky were the first, and they're both still with us. Soon after, Mark Doherty, who became one of my best friends, started waiting tables, then managing, and ended up working at the restaurant for seventeen years. I've always promoted from within. Staff loyalty is a two-way street, and I'm proud that these guys and many others—like prep cooks Jaime and Antonio—have been with Davio's for a long time.

I knew that a huge part of a restaurant's success rested in the hands of its team members, and I began valuing each one and letting them know how much I appreciated his or her work. The success of Davio's today comes from our people, there's no question.

～

I put in plenty of sixteen-hour days that first year, but I never minded it: I found that I was in love with what I was doing. I had dreamed about owning my own place all my life, and now I actually had four thousand square feet—on Newbury Street, no less, the coolest location in Boston. I loved that it was a romantic, cozy space with a New York feel. The downstairs portion, which had been used as a restaurant, had two rooms seating eighty at tables that were close together and intimate. The walls were brick, and a red velvet curtain hung from a brass rod that ran along the lower half of the walls. There was even a patio out front.

I was also cheered by a sense that the challenges I was facing were ultimately manageable. The deal I negotiated had been a good one, enabling me to pay the bills while I stabilized operations. At $3,500 a month, the lease was low, and my quick transformation of the upstairs bar into a lucrative casual pizza and pasta cafe brought in money. The old owners had only been doing about $500 a week upstairs; within a year of opening, we increased that to about $25,000! It was a phenomenal boon for Davio's. After we installed a round neon sign in the window that read PIZZA AND PASTA, it exploded with guests almost overnight.

The sign's shape was similar to that of the Davio's sign in front of the restaurant—a rather tacky, ball-like thing. We had to put the cafe sign in the window because the city's architectural committee wouldn't allow it on the street. Once it was up, people were saying, "Wow, Davio's serves pizza!" and flocking to the place. You have to remember, this was before chains like Bertucci's or California Pizza Kitchen were big, before gourmet pizza was widely available. Nobody was serving great pizza like ours.

To keep people coming in during those tough early weeks, I also lowered prices downstairs. The restaurant was very expensive, which I thought was ridiculous. Dishes were as high as the Ritz, but this was a small Italian restaurant. Within the first week of taking over the place, I did an inventory of food costs and found them very low, which is to say the guests were not getting a good value. I reduced prices about 25 percent across the board. The restaurant was still considered expensive, but guests were now getting a somewhat better value, and it made a difference.

⌒

With our personnel and finances headed in a much better direction, I finally was able to begin creating the kind of food I had always wanted to offer in the downstairs restaurant. At the time, most Boston restaurants were pretty similar. If you were a steakhouse, you served the same steak, chops, shrimp cocktails, and baked stuffed shrimp. If you were an Italian restaurant, you served mostly premade, red-sauced casserole dishes like lasagna, veal and eggplant parm, manicotti, and cannelloni, in addition to other baked pastas, like Alfredos. I'd grown up with these Italian-American standards and loved them, but they weren't what I wanted to serve at Davio's.

I was on fire about new, lighter sauces and fresh, made-to-order dishes that so many of us young American chefs were inspired to create at the time. Not only was this a beautiful cuisine that I loved and wanted to serve, but I realized that I could grab a competitive edge if I made the food at Davio's original and unique. This is old news today, but at the time it was cutting edge and part of my vision for the place. I had been especially inspired by the food at Allegro in Waltham, Massachusetts, prepared by one of Boston's first great chef-owners, Jimmy Burke. Like the rest of us, Jimmy was heavily influenced by French nouvelle cuisine, even though his food was Italian. His light sauces, al dente pasta, and simple, fresh dishes reflected the principles of what was then spreading across the United States as the New American Cuisine.

And the thing was, you couldn't get Jimmy's food any-where but at his restaurant. This is exactly what I wanted for Davio's.

Within six months after I took over—by the time the *Boston Globe* reviewed Davio's and changed my life—we had an entirely new, original menu in place. I wanted the menu to be a team effort and had asked each chef to suggest recipes. The kitchen by this time included Tommy Golden, a very innovative chef I hired after seeing that we needed more creativity on the line. We all worked together to refine the menu, dish by dish. By the time we were finished, you couldn't get any of Davio's dishes—like our penne with smoked chicken and sun-dried tomatoes—anywhere but *at Davio's*.

Another element I changed, in my effort to set a powerful new tone, was the dress code. Remember dress codes? Initially, the one at Davio's was pretty strict. Men were supposed to wear jackets and weren't allowed to wear jeans and sneakers. I thought that was crazy. This was the mid-'80s. The amazingly springy Reeboks and Nikes we're all so used to now had been available for only five or six years. They were in style. People loved them. Why ban them from the restaurant?

Jeff Gates, my star server, thought I was going too far. I didn't care. "This isn't the Ritz-Carlton," I said. "This is a tiny Italian restaurant. Let people wear sneakers. Will it kill us?"

The Four Seasons had just opened about eight blocks away, and even though it was expensive, it wasn't as formal as the Ritz. Lots of rock stars and celebrities were starting to stay there. It was clear to me that Americans were becoming more casual. I'd also seen evidence of this when I'd visited upscale restaurants in Los Angeles and San Francisco. I knew a different breed of diner had cropped up with money to spend, and I wanted to cater to them. We no longer had to exclude people that weren't part of the old guard in jackets and ties.

I'll never forget, the first month, a couple came in and ordered a $250 bottle of wine, with a total bill of about $500. Jeff came over to me and said, "Man, Steve, you were so right. That guy is wearing sneakers."

"Yup," I said. "And he's staying at the Four Seasons."

In transforming Davio's that first year, I ultimately wanted to shift the general service ethic. I wanted ours to be an upbeat place known around the city for putting guests at the center of the experience. To me, this was the mark of great hospitality and a massive departure from the old Davio's. To set this in stone, I continually encouraged the staff to come to me with any special requests a guest had that they didn't know how to handle.

One day, I got a call from somebody in Stevie Ray Vaughan's camp saying the musician was coming in that night. He was on a special diet, and the person asked if we'd cook some of his food for him.

"Sure," I said. "What is it?"

"Well, it's a rabbit," the guy responded.

"A rabbit?"

"Yeah, a rabbit. We'll send it over. You know how to cook a rabbit?"

"Yeah. We'll slow roast it."

An hour later, they sent over a rabbit loin. It weighed a couple pounds. I'd cooked a rabbit or two in culinary school, but this was Stevie Ray Vaughan, so I called my teacher, Roberta, just to make sure that braising it was the way to go. It was, and I cooked the thing really slowly. Vaughan loved it; he thought Davio's was great. The old owners had been so arrogant about their food that they never would have accommodated Vaughan's request. We did, and Vaughan became just the first of many celebrities who would dine with us over the years. Tragically, he died a couple of years later in a helicopter crash. At least the rabbit didn't get him.

Within a year my beautiful little restaurant was much changed. There was no drug use (that I saw), and the staff was treating each other and the guests well. The food was fantastic and unique, business was thriving, and great reviews had put us on the map. The restaurant was also looking good because we had enough money coming in to make substantial improvements. We replaced the old ceiling with a beautiful tin one and had the booths reupholstered and treated with fabric protector. Sometimes, after a great day, I had to pinch myself to believe how far we had come. It was a heady time at Davio's and the start of everything we were to become. It was a fun time, too. The staff was happy—not from cocaine, but from doing a good job and making good money. What partying there was took place after hours.

Some shenanigans did still happen. One of our servers, Tracy, was a pretty redhead who was totally open about her sexuality. Everybody wanted her, and she seemed to do her best to oblige. One morning, I came in early and found that Tommy the bartender was already there. We were easing into the day with cups of coffee when he told me, smiling ear to ear, that he had finally done the deed with Tracy at 3:00 a.m. that morning.

"Where did that happen?" I asked.

He nodded across the restaurant. "Right over there. Table 7."

Hey, I was the owner and I suppose I should have been bothered, but things were different then, and I didn't do everything right. Sure, as the boss I had fired people, hired people, and done the hard stuff, but we were still young and having fun. And Tommy was so good at what he did; he brought so much business into the restaurant. I think I high-fived him.

But that wasn't the end of the story. Later that day, before dinner service, Jeff was spot cleaning the upholstery when he came across a spot he couldn't get rid of. I half-noticed him across the room scrubbing away for what seemed like half an hour before giving up in frustration.

"Steve, this cleaner stuff was a rip-off," he said.

"What do you mean?"

"It's bogus. It doesn't work."

"What are you talking about? What's the problem?"

"It doesn't get the job done. It just will not touch this spot!" He pointed out a couple of strange, dark, circular stains on the banquet at Table 7. "Look, I've rubbed it and rubbed it— rubbed the hell out of it—but it just isn't going away."

I told Jeff what exactly it was he was cleaning. "Ew, gross!" he screamed and ran to the bathroom; he stayed in there another twenty minutes washing his hands. But I'll say this: He was right. That stain wasn't going anywhere. And neither was Davio's.

Restaurant Lessons to Live By

Any business owner must be able to lead. Ask yourself if you have the personality for it. If not, you might try another line of work.

Establishing trust is fundamental to all business relationships. Visit your vendors and other partners. Get to know them. Let them get to know you.

Know your strengths and use them to their fullest, but hire the right people to help you out in other areas.

Promote from within. Loyalty between management and team members is a two-way street.

You don't have to be perfect. Sometimes, when you're young and crazy, you can overlook what happens at 3:00 a.m. at Table 7.

CHAPTER THREE

It's All About the Guest

In December 2012 I got an e-mail from a woman who had parked in the garage below our Boston location. Upon returning home, she was shocked to discover that she'd lost her purse. She couldn't find it anywhere and was freaking out. As it turned out, Nancy, one of our bartenders, had found the purse lying around in the garage as she was going to her car. She had opened it up, hoping to find out information about its owner so she could return it. She discovered the woman's name and address, but the woman's cell phone was inside the purse, so Nancy couldn't call her.

At most restaurants, team members who find items left behind shrug their shoulders and wait for the owner to come claim what was lost (or even worse, keep the item for themselves). That's not what Nancy did here, for a woman who was not even a guest. Somehow, Nancy was able to get the woman's landline number. She got the woman on the phone. "Don't worry, I'll bring the purse over to you."

This woman lived in Quincy, about twenty-five minutes south of Boston. It was far out of Nancy's way, but she trucked right over there and delivered the purse. When the grateful woman offered money as a reward, Nancy declined. "No, no. You just pass it along to someone else. Do something good for someone like I did for you, and I'll feel good."

The woman had written to tell me how blown away she was at the service Nancy had provided. She hadn't eaten yet at Davio's, but now she was definitely going to come in. Reading her effusive praise, I wanted to throw sexual harassment laws to the wind and give Nancy a big hug. Service like that—for our guests and everyone else—is what Davio's is all about. We go to extraordinary lengths to please people. Why? Because we love our guests and take pleasure in making people happy. But we also love making money. If guests aren't delighted, they're not coming back. If they are delighted, they'll not only come back—they'll tell their friends. Our dual mission statement, which we ask all team members to memorize, says it all: "To provide the quality of service, so that our guests will purchase, come back, and purchase again. To develop and maintain a sense of pride in our restaurant, and a friendly and professional attitude towards our guests and each other."

The most interesting thing about this little episode, I think, is how ordinary it is for us. Sure, we screw up sometimes, and guests let us know. But I get far more reports like this one. We go to extremes for all guests all the time—and if you're starting a restaurant, I strongly encourage you to do the same.

If someone comes into our Boston location asking for littleneck clams on their pasta and we don't have them, we don't say, "No, sorry. We can't do that for you." We go out right then and there to Legal Sea Foods down the street and get them special for our guest (we choose Legal's because they have the best quality). Ask for a bone-in, forty-eight-ounce prime rib eye, a special cut we don't normally serve, and we'll stop in on another local restaurant, Grill 23, which uses the same Brandt meat we do. We did this not long ago for Dwayne "The Rock" Johnson when he was in Boston filming a movie. Back in the '20s and '30s, a famous restaurant called the Palm used to provide this level of service. When I heard about it, I knew we had to do it, too.

I don't ask just my team members to go to extremes; I do it myself, too. I was driving home one night when my phone rang. It was Joe Torre, then manager of the Los Angeles Dodgers and a previous guest in Boston. "Hey, Stevie. Our team's in Philadelphia; we're playing the Phillies. It's the playoffs and we're staying at the Westin hotel. I noticed there's a Davio's across the street. Does that have anything to do with you?"

"Yeah, Joe," I said. "That's my restaurant."

"Oh, great. I'm going to bring my whole crew there tomorrow night. Are you gonna be there?"

"Of course. Where else am I going to be?"

I had no plans to be in Philly. I was supposed to be in Boston. But I didn't hesitate to cancel everything and fly straight to Philly. It cost me $600, but I had to go. An important guest had specifically requested it. And good thing: Torre brought all the coaches. And then every night for the next three nights, he brought his family and a lot of players. We got thousands of dollars of added revenue, not to mention the good it did for our brand. It was fantastic!

A much more routine thing I do to please guests is to act as their concierge. Guests come up to me all the time saying things like, "Oh, I know you're the restaurant guy. I'm going to New York next week. Can you get me into Nobu?" My automatic response: "Sure, what time do you need it for?" Or they'll call at odd hours asking me to get them VIP tickets to the New England Patriots, or seeking advice on how to roast a chicken. My wife thinks I'm crazy to fulfill requests like these. The more I do, she says, the more people will call me for favors. It'll be an avalanche! I know she's right, but I don't care. I'll do anything to please my guests. (Well, almost anything. I won't do anything illegal, like sell alcohol after the legal closing time—a request I often get. I'll also take your keys if you've had too much to drink.)

You don't have to be famous for me to make special accommodations for you, either. The other night, I was in the restaurant when Tonino said that the guests at Table 71 wanted to meet me. I agreed to come over, but then I got busy and forgot to do it. Around 10:00 p.m. I left for home. I had driven about twenty minutes, was about halfway there, when I said, "Oh, man, I forgot to see those people!" I didn't hesitate for a minute. I got off the highway, turned right around (half getting lost in the process), and got back to the restaurant around 10:45. I wound up sitting and chatting with the guests for another hour. And this was after a fourteen-hour day! I was tired, but these guests had been to the restaurant before, and they wanted to meet me. This kind of thing is just something you do in our business.

It's just as important to pay attention to the thousand little preferences that guests have. As I mentioned in the last chapter, all of us, myself included, go out of our way to log and track guest desires in our computer. Every day, I go into the database and check out who is coming in and what special treatment they request. When they come back again, they find that we've magically remembered from the last time. Do you know how cool that is to them? "How did you know I like that table?" they'll exclaim in amazement. I just laugh. "Well, we keep track of what you like." No detail is too small: the temperature at which guests prefer their wine, the way they're used to having their steak cooked (some people order medium, but they really mean well done). If you're a regular at our Boston restaurant, you can go into Davio's in Atlanta and we'll still sit you right close to the bar, because we know that's just the way you want it. This gives us a huge advantage over our competition. Why would you go to Davio's in Boston if you live in Philadelphia? A lot of people wouldn't remain that loyal, but they are loyal to us because they know they'll be treated like a local no matter which of our restaurants they visit.

I've talked so far about the lengths we go to in order to handle special requests and to provide the very best experience possible. But all of this rests on something even more fundamental: basic standards of conduct. If you want to really provide superior service, you have to start from a higher place. The baseline of conduct in your restaurant has to be oriented around treating people properly and with respect. If you don't establish clear rules about how to behave around guests, what good is it to have nice bathrooms and silverware? And how will you ever find yourself automatically turning around when you're halfway home to sit with yet another table that has requested it?

We have many standards of conduct at Davio's; most of these are stated in our team member manual and covered in our staff training programs. A big one is pretty simple: Make eye contact with guests as much as possible. It's the best way to connect with them and understand what they want. Another standard is what your mom might have told you growing up: If you see it, fix it! The total appearance of the restaurant is everyone's responsibility. If something is out of place or needs cleaning or repair, don't just wait for someone else to do it; fix it yourself. At Davio's you'll see multiple people running to clean up a broken plate, or napkins promptly folded and placed on chairs when guests get up to go to the bathroom. A third policy we have—that many restaurants seemingly don't—is no cell phone use on the premises. Actually, it's not just using cellphones; we don't let our team members wear or carry them while in the restaurant, on the clock, or in view of guests. When we're serving guests, our job is to focus *all* our attention on them. Guests need to know that our staff members are taking care of them, not worrying about their boyfriends or what they and their friends are going to be doing later that night.

Another big standard has to do with how we greet guests when they come in. I can't stand it when I go into a restaurant and the server greets me with a huge smile and says, "Hi! I'm Nicole!" It's artificial. Diners don't care what the server's name is. And the server doesn't really care about the diner's name. It's not that kind of relationship. It's about service, not friendship. My family gets upset at me because whenever a server introduces herself, I'll react by introducing everyone in our party one by one. "Hi, I'm Steve. And this is Pam. And that's Max and Ella."

"Do you really have to do that, Dad?" Ella asks.

And then, of course, throughout the entire meal I'll make a point of addressing Nicole by her name. "Nicole, can I have more butter? Nicole, can we get the check? Thanks, Nicole!" I can't help myself—this just irritates me so much! At Davio's our standard of service is *not* to introduce ourselves by name—to keep it formal and fun, but not excessively or inappropriately friendly. Of course, if guests do ask, we'll say our names; it's not like we're spying for the government or anything.

While I'm on the subject of pet peeves, let me ask you something. Doesn't it drive you crazy when you sit down at a table and the server smells like he's just been smoking out by the dumpster? It drives me crazy, which is why we have a non-negotiable standard of no smoking at any time during a shift. But let's say your server does smell great. What if he reads you the specials off a card or cheat sheet? Doesn't that seem unprofessional? Shouldn't he take his job seriously enough to know the food inside and out? When I see that happen at another restaurant I'm visiting, I'm appalled. I don't blame the server as much as I do the manager and owner for allowing this to happen. They're showing a lack of commitment to their business—a "let it slide" type of attitude. At Davio's, if one of our servers doesn't memorize the specials, I want to know about it, because that's yet another standard I insist on.

A final standard I'll mention among the dozens, even hundreds we have involves what we do when guests *aren't* happy. We don't just give you a free dessert or a discount—we also take the item off the bill. We're really good about that. We don't want to hear that something about the dining experience was "okay." We want to hear that it was excellent—that you loved it—and we'll do whatever it takes to make it right. When guests e-mail me with complaints, and we did make a mistake, we'll invite them to come back in for a free dinner or even offer them a $50 or $100 gift card, depending on how bad the mistake was. I want them to try us again, to give us a chance to make it right. The way I figure it, every person who isn't happy will tell several of his or her friends, and those friends tell their friends, and before we know it we'll have a whole lot of people saying bad things about Davio's—from one slipup.

There's even more at stake with every service encounter these days because of social media. Can I vent for a moment about Yelp and other online guest response sites? I hate them! So many people are quick to post negative comments when they perceive they weren't treated right. That hits every restaurant hard, and it isn't fair. If we didn't please you, tell *us* about it first (in person, on our website, or by contacting me directly at steve@davios.com) so that we have a chance to fix the problem and make amends.

On Yelp, anybody can post negative comments, including competitors and disgruntled ex-team members, and the damage is done—even when there is another side to the story, or when the criticism is just plain wrong. Peoples' livelihoods are affected. At Davio's we're bent on pleasing people, so if anything is wrong, we most definitely do want to know about it. Would you believe that I actually watch dirty plates come back as tables are being cleared to see if guests didn't finish their food? When I notice that someone didn't touch their plate, I'll go to the table myself and ask if anything was wrong.

If you do like posting comments on social media, we have someone on our staff, Tania, who monitors all the big sites every day, responding to good comments and bad. Listening and fixing—that's a huge standard of service we take seriously.

~~

You might say I'm taking it too far. Is it really necessary to have so many standards, or to note that Peter Wolf of the J. Geils Band likes us to make baked potatoes special for him, or to fly out to Philly just because Joe Torre wants me to come for dinner? From my perspective, these kinds of questions are the real problem. We in the restaurant business usually don't do *enough*. When I look around the restaurant scene, it shocks me how many people don't get *in their bones* the importance of pleasing guests. I can't tell you how many times I've seen servers, bartenders, or cooks complain about this guest who asked us to cook the chicken without the sauce, or that guest who wanted a different table, or a third guest who thought the room temperature was too cold, or a fourth guest who wanted an item not on the menu. Guest preferences and requests are endless, and a lot of staff members don't like it. My view: Get over it! It's not our position to judge what guests ask for. It's not about us—it's about our guests. We're in the hospitality business. We're here to serve. We're here to show respect. We're here to satisfy peoples' quirks and not ask questions. The guest really *is* always right.

And another thing. You may not want to hear this, Mr. or Ms. Budding Restaurateur, but offering superior service to guests means being willing to change virtually anything about your restaurant if your guests demand it. Many people in my business work for someone else for years and think,

"When I have my own place, *this* is what I'm going to do. I'll finally do it my way." They refuse to consider how guests might feel about it—and they pay the price. One talented but arrogant chef I know initially proclaimed that he was going to do his food his way, period. If you had asked him to make you a simple burger, he would have told you to get up and leave. Fifteen years later, ask him for that burger, and he'll jump to make it for you. You can start with an idea of your own, but you have to be willing to respond to guests. Otherwise, you're dead. Times change, and you have to change with them. It's just reality.

In 1985 we didn't have meatballs on our menu. No way, I said. Meatballs are an American invention; they're not Italian. Back when my grandmother arrived, she and her fellow immigrants were so poor they couldn't afford decent meat. They'd buy the worst cuts and cook them all day in sauce. That's where meatballs come from. And veal parm is no better. In Italy they make eggplant parm, but in America the immigrants again took these tough pieces of veal, pounded the hell out of them, and slathered them with sauce and cheese to make them edible. I didn't want any of it in my upscale restaurant. I wanted people to come to Davio's for our own food. We'd create our own special recipes people couldn't buy anywhere else. Was I a little arrogant? Yes, I was.

Fast-forward twenty years. Meatballs are acceptable in upscale restaurants. People love them. The best restaurants make them. Did I bury my head in the sand and refuse to put them on the menu? No. Well, initially I did, but then my chefs Eric and Steve talked me into it. "Steve," they said, "I think we have to do meatballs."

"Oh my God!" I said.

Finally, I gave in and showed the guys how to make them like my mom did. Working together, we tweaked the recipe, substituting Kobe beef for normal ground beef. Today, we sell more meatballs than you can imagine—probably thirty to forty orders a day in each restaurant. We still bill ourselves as a "Northern Italian restaurant." I can guarantee you that there are no meatballs in Northern Italy. Just thinking about serving them would have once seemed crazy to me. I'm sorry I have to write about it in this book. But it's not about me. It's about the guests.

Now, there are limits to how much we can change. In any business you shouldn't compromise the core of who or what you are in order to please guests—you shouldn't destroy your brand. I could introduce meatballs in our Boston restaurant because by the 2000s the Davio's brand was already well established in the local area. I could—and did—go even further and sell Philly cheese steak spring rolls there. How is *that* Northern Italian? When we open restaurants in new cities, we specifically don't include spring rolls on our main dinner menu, because we feel we need to set the tone and establish a clear brand identity. Once that brand identity is there, we have more freedom to change with the times and our guests' evolving desires.

Even when you're well established, you certainly shouldn't try to please everyone. One of our guests asked why we didn't serve nachos at our bar. I just couldn't go there; it's not what we do. Nachos are Mexican. There is no such thing as Italian nachos. It's crazy! Other guests write me e-mails complaining that we're too expensive. They ask why we can't offer cheap steak for under $20 rather than the prime meat we serve.

Davio's Kobe Meatballs and Marinara Sauce

You want meatballs? Okay, here goes. You need a good marinara sauce on hand in order to cook meatballs, so let's start there.

Put **3 tablespoons extra virgin olive oil** (Monini preferred) in a saucepan and warm over medium heat. Then add **½ cup finely chopped Spanish onion** and sauté until translucent. Add **3 finely chopped cloves fresh garlic** and cook until the garlic is a light golden color. Whatever you do, don't overcook the garlic! Then add **1 cup white wine** to deglaze the pan. Continue to cook the garlic until the liquid is reduced by half, about 3 or 4 minutes. Next, pour in **4 (28-ounce) cans of Italian San Marzano tomatoes** that you've crushed by hand. Add **salt and pepper** to taste. Bring the sauce to a boil, stir, and reduce heat to a simmer. Let the sauce simmer uncovered for 1 hour, stirring every 10 minutes. Remove from heat and add **2 tablespoons unsalted butter** and **¼ cup chiffonade fresh basil leaves.** Congratulations: You now have some killer sauce to work with.

Next come the meatballs. In a large bowl soak **1 loaf of stale bread,** broken into small pieces, in **2 cups whole milk** for 2 hours. Over medium-high heat, sauté **1 diced white onion** and **2 diced cloves garlic**. Add the sautéed onions and garlic to the soaked bread and combine with **¼ cup extra virgin olive oil** (Monini preferred), **2 pounds ground Kobe beef, 2 pounds ground veal, 2 pounds ground pork, ½ cup grated Parmigiano cheese, ½ cup grated Romano cheese, ½ cup chopped parsley, ½ cup chopped basil**, and **6 whole eggs.** Mix all this stuff together, cover the bowl with plastic wrap, and refrigerate overnight.

The next day, take the bowl out of the refrigerator and form the mixture into approximately 20 (3-ounce) balls. Over medium-high heat in a large pan, cook the meatballs in **¼ cup extra virgin olive oil** (Monini preferred) for 10 minutes, making sure that the meatballs are spread out in the pan and don't touch one another. Turn them often so they don't burn. Remove the meatballs from the pan and cool. Place the cooled meatballs in another large pan and cover them with **¾ of a gallon of the marinara sauce** you made earlier. Wrap the pan with plastic wrap, and refrigerate it overnight. The next day, cook the meatballs and sauce for at least 3 hours at 325 degrees before serving.

P.S. Does that sound too long? Let's strike a deal: If after an hour you just can't take the smell any longer and have to dig in, that's fine, too.

P.P.S. You can cook the meatballs in the sauce immediately after sautéing, but I really do recommend letting them sit overnight.

Again, it's not what we do. We're about quality meat at reasonable (but not inexpensive) prices. At a certain point you have to listen to your inner compass, stick to your vision, and do the best that you can with each guest. So long as you can honestly say to yourself, "I really did go as far as possible to please this person," it's okay—you've done enough.

~

Wait a minute, I take that back. You haven't done enough. You've barely started. Because making "It's all about the guest" a reality isn't just about pleasing individual guests in the moment. *It's about thinking through every single business decision you make from this point of view*—or at least every decision that impacts the guest experience. I mean *every* decision, big and small. Let me give you a few examples, starting with the least glamorous and proceeding from there.

OUR BATHROOMS. Why do we outfit them with granite countertops? Why do we have small, self-contained rooms with toilets in them instead of just standard stalls? Why do we have thick maple doors and stainless steel sink basins? Because our guests want these things. You have no idea how many people e-mail me to say, "Wow, you guys have great bathrooms." Our guests come from homes that have nice bathrooms, and they appreciate the same in the restaurants they frequent. So even though it costs us hundreds of thousands of dollars to doll up our bathrooms, we're going to go the extra mile. We also make our staff use the same bathroom as our guests. We want them in there all the time, because we figure that way they'll keep them cleaner. Guests also see our team members in the bathroom, and assume that it must be clean, since the staff is using it.

OUR CHAIRS. I don't like it when I go to a restaurant and feel uncomfortable. I want a nice, well-designed, soft chair to sit on, and I know most guests do, too. Our Shelby Williams chairs cost $450 apiece. They're well made—nice enough that I would put them in my own house. In fact, they're *more* expensive than the Pottery Barn chairs I have in my house. But our guests deserve them, and we can afford to provide them.

OUR WINEGLASSES. Of course, we can't afford everything. As a businessperson I want tough glassware, because breakage costs us a lot of money. Glasses break all the time on our hardwood and tile floors. (Unlike many restaurants, we don't use mats in our kitchens because I find them extremely dirty and greasy. I challenge you to ever find a single mat. If I saw one, I'd freak out!) So we chose our glasses because they're tough *and* they look good. They have long, elegant stems so that you can grip them without the heat from your hand warming up your wine. Could we have bought more expensive glasses? Maybe, but they would have broken all the time. Often, you have to find a happy medium between pleasing the guest and doing what's necessary to run a viable business. (By the way, unlike most restaurants, we don't use soda guns in our mixed drinks. We use bottle service and fresh juices, even though it's more expensive, because they make the drinks taste better. We also purify our water for coffee, ice, and other uses using the well-regarded AquaHealth purification system.)

When a lot of restaurants open, they have the most expensive glasses and beautiful china. Go back in six months, and you'll find that all that is gone and you're back to plain

American white plates. That's because restaurants beat up their tableware, and so they can't sustain the extreme cost of the very best. You want guests to be happy, but not *too* happy. Let me put it another way: How happy will your guests be when you're out of business and they have nowhere to go? I say maintain a balance, taking guests and their needs as the starting point of the calculation, and you'll be fine.

OUR SILVERWARE. You ever pick up a knife or fork at a restaurant and find that it's light as air? Not at Davio's. Our silverware is not only beautiful—it's also heavy, substantial. People like a heavy knife when they're slicing into their steaks. I know I do. And I like a big fork, too. You can't serve a $46 steak and give guests a flimsy knife to cut it with. We used to use wooden steak knives, but they looked funky after being washed so many times. I know our guests like our silverware because they sometimes run off with it. Especially our steak knives. Now, we could purchase $50 or even $100 knives for our guests, but once again, you have to reach a good balance. Our guests might enjoy the more expensive knives, but they also appreciate the ones we currently have—and so do we.

OUR TELEVISIONS. If you walk around our dining room, you'll notice no TVs in sight. We do have flat-screen TVs, but we keep them on one side of the bar, away from the dining room. Why? When I go out for dinner with family and friends, I don't want to have a TV staring me in the face. You can't have much of a conversation when your friend or husband or business associate is watching TV at the same time as they're trying to talk to you. Our guests feel the same. Because we're not a sports bar but rather an upscale dining restaurant, I want people to come here and enjoy being with other people.

At the same time, I respect our guests enough to want to give them a choice. If they come here and really do want to watch the game while they eat, we have a place for that. But it's a small place, because only a small minority of our guests want to watch-and-eat. The exception is when the local football team is playing in the championship game. Then we'll wheel in four or five large-screen TVs just for the day—again, because our guests want it.

OUR MENU. I've talked about meatballs and spring rolls, but let me say a word about our menu size. It would be easier and cheaper for us to include fewer items. Why do we have so many? Because guests like choices. They want ten different meat dishes to select from, ten different fish dishes, ten different kinds of pasta. At Davio's you can come in with people who are vegan, gluten intolerant, vegetarian, or lactose intolerant and everyone will have great, high-quality items to choose from—it's part of what makes it fun to eat with us. If you can't eat gluten, we even give you an entire menu to explore. Recognizing that cost is an issue for some people, we also include some items that aren't nearly as expensive as our $46 steak.

You get the idea. Every single decision you make in a restaurant, big and small, has to be about the guest. If that's not your orientation, if you're all about cheap or you're all about you, than you should think about getting into another business. You also need to keep reviewing and updating your business decisions to make sure you're doing the very best you can for your guests. The work is never done. I personally research and test all of our products—our pasta, our olive oil, our meat, our fish. I don't tell our chefs to just handle it; I want to be part of the decision myself.

Take our pasta as an example. During our first year we made it all fresh, but I soon got frustrated at how mushy it was. I like my pasta al dente—the only way my mom ever made it. So we switched to imported Italian dry pasta, with the exception of our gnocchi and ravioli, which we continued to make fresh. Twenty-eight years later, pasta technology is better than ever, and we've been able to find a $5,000 machine made in Italy that spits out the very best fresh pasta that can also be cooked al dente. All of our restaurants have these machines now.

When it comes to the guest experience, every decision is a big one.

There was one evening in 2003 that I'll never forget. We had moved our main Boston restaurant from its original location on Newbury to the much larger space on Arlington Street where it currently is. Initially, I knew almost everyone who came into the new place, just as I had for years at the old place. My practice had always been to circulate during meal-times, babysit the tables, give them my personal attention. On this night, nine months after our reopening, the place was packed, with a long waiting list. I looked out at the 250 people dining with us and turned to Joe B., our manager. "Joe, wow. Look around. Look at the tables! Look at the bar!"

He seemed puzzled. "What?"

"I don't know a single guest here. Not one person. They have no idea who I am."

I didn't know anyone because we had grown and were attracting a whole new clientele that had never been to Davio's before. The beautiful restaurant, the big bar, the open kitchen, the great food—all of it was working. But the most important thing of all was working, too: the way we took care of guests. I had laid down standards for service and hired people like our bartender Nancy, who not merely abided by the rules but surpassed them in incredible ways. Our service was known to the wider community; it had become part of our established brand. This was the day that I knew Davio's had made it, because "It's all about the guest" had surpassed me and become organizational. If I had a heart attack and died, the restaurant would continue on without me, pleasing guests just as it always had.

I'm not dead yet, and until I am, guests will get my full attention. Not long ago, New England Patriots quarterback Tom Brady ate dinner in our Boston restaurant with his family. A week or so later, he had a big game coming up, so on the Friday before the game, I sent him a text: "Tom, you guys gonna come in tonight? If not, I'll bring dinner to you. My treat."

I knew that on Saturdays the Patriots stay in a hotel, so Friday was the last night before the game that Tom would get to be at home with his family. Given how famous Tom is, it is hard for them to go out for dinner very often. That's why I offered to bring the food to him. He texted me right back: "Steve, that would be great. Is 6:30 p.m. good?"

I asked the chefs to make up some rib eyes, some filets, and a bunch of other things I know Tom likes. Tom's house was a five-minute drive from the restaurant, so I decided I would deliver it myself. At 6:15 I went to the garage for my car, food in hand, only to find that someone had blocked me in. I asked around the garage, but nobody knew whose car it was—I was totally stuck!

I didn't know what to do. It was just about 6:30. If I didn't get a ride soon, I would arrive too late and the food would be ruined. I couldn't walk because it would take me fifteen minutes and it was twenty degrees out. Then one of the engineers for the building came out. I screamed to him, "Kevin! Kevin! You've got to help me out! I have a food delivery. Can you take me real quick?"

He shook his head. "Steve, I've got to be home. My wife is gonna kill me."

"Please, can you give me a ride? You'll be happy you did."

He thought about it for a moment. "All right, all right. Throw the food in my truck."

As we drove, Kevin gave me an elbow. "Steve, what are you doing delivering food? Don't you have people to do that?"

"Kev," I told him, "we're going to Tom Brady's house."

He looked over at me. "Don't bullshit me."

"No really," I insisted, "you're going to meet him in five minutes." Then he freaked out. "Oh, my God! Oh, my God! I'm gonna meet Tom Brady!"

It was 6:45 p.m. when we pulled up. The food was still hot, and Tom was incredibly grateful. "I can't believe you did this. You saved us. Thank you so much for bringing the food over."

We said our good-byes, and Kevin was over-the-moon happy. "Wow. I can't believe I just met Tom Brady. Tom Brady!"

I had hoped that my gesture would produce another Super Bowl visit for my favorite team. Unfortunately, two days later the Patriots had the worst second-half performance I'd ever seen at Gillette Stadium. Still, I'm glad I made the extra effort. Pleasing guests is what we do. And the thrill of doing it never gets old.

Restaurant Lessons to Live By

If you're starting a business, be prepared to go to extremes for guests—each and every day.

You and your team members can provide superior service only if you start from a higher place, and that means having clear standards.

Addressing guest complaints should be a core part of any company's service culture.

Listen to your guests and provide what they want—even if you don't like it. But do make sure to stay true to your brand.

Serving guests isn't just about pleasing them in the moment. It's about thinking through every business decision that affects the guest experience.

CHAPTER FOUR

Pay Attention!
Mentors Are Everywhere

Have I told you yet about the time Julia Child slept with me?

It happened in 1996. I pulled up to her house in Cambridge, Massachusetts, to take her to a charity event we were attending in Providence. That city's mayor, Buddy Cianci, was honoring her, and I had been asked to serve as her escort.

By this point Julia was in her mid-eighties, and we had been acquainted for many years. I had gone to other events with her and enjoyed chatting with her, but I had never gotten a chance to talk to her one-on-one and really get to know her.

I peppered her with questions from the moment she got in the car. It was rainy and dark, and for the first few minutes she was right there—my childhood idol—firing answers back. Then, before we hit the highway, she didn't respond for a minute. I looked over, and she was asleep.

"Jesus Christ," I said to myself. "How disappointing."

Not to be too crude, but it was like being after a girl and finally getting her in your bed—only to have her fall asleep.

When we arrived I woke her up. "Okay, we're here, Julia."

She opened her purse, powdered her nose and her cheeks, and applied a thick coat of red lipstick. Then we went in and she came instantly alive. She greeted everyone enthusiastically: the front-of-house people, the event people, several guests who noticed her. And then she made a beeline for the back. "I want to see the kitchen! I want to meet everybody!"

Now, I've hosted many famous chefs, foodies, and others at Davio's over the years, and no one else has ever done what Julia did in that kitchen. She greeted every single person—the chefs, the salad guys, the dishwashers, the pastry chef, asking and answering question after question. Ten minutes earlier, she'd been asleep, but now she was up and giving these people her full attention. She was having the time of her life. She knew who she was, and she loved being that person.

We all ate dinner together and had a fun evening. When it was time for us to leave, I thought to myself, *Okay, my time for questions—here I go!* But once again, before we even made it to the highway, she fell asleep. That was okay. I had already learned a restaurant lesson that I will never forget: The most important thing you can give people is your time and attention.

I'd been watching Julia since I was fourteen and I knew all her dishes, but nothing has taught me as much or served me as powerfully in my career as watching her give herself to everybody that night.

~

Julia and I became friends. She had been to the restaurant a few times, but now she came more frequently, giving us some great publicity. Our staff members were shocked to see newspapers mentioning our relationship. "How cool, she knows Steve!" they exclaimed. Julia would call us up and say, "Make sure you tell Steve I'm coming tonight!" I'd drop everything to be there, first because I still couldn't believe I was friends with Julia Child, and also, you never knew when a pearl of wisdom would drop from her mouth. Eat everything, but in moderation, she told me. Eat many courses, but make them small. She always complained that the portions at Davio's were too big, although she loved our food, especially our angel hair pasta with pomodoro sauce. I knew that American guests expected large portions because they wanted to feel like they were getting a good value. So, although I appreciated her opinion, our portion sizes stayed the same. (It's all about the guest, right?)

Today, Julia is gone, but I think of her fondly as an important mentor in my life. Mentors are everything. It's hard to make it in restaurants—or anything else—if you don't have them. Why? Because none of us are born geniuses. It's arrogant to think we know everything. I hate to say it, but some business owners (the ones I'm not friends with) *are* arrogant. Pigheaded. Basically, not nice. Like fourteen-year-old kids, they rebel against anybody older and wiser. They don't know how to listen. And that's too bad. Running a company is tough, and you need to listen and learn if you are to have any hope of making it. So if you're starting a new venture and you don't think you need a mentor, think again. Stop what you're doing and go out and get one right now!

Julia Child's Favorite Angel Hair Pomodoro

This dish is simple and *so* good. In a medium saucepan, heat **2 ounces extra virgin olive oil** (Monini preferred) over medium-high heat. Take **1 large garlic clove,** slice it paper thin, add it to the oil, and cook for about 1 minute or until the garlic is golden brown. Now add **16 ounces whole San Marzano tomatoes** to the garlic and cook them for 5 to 6 minutes. You want to simmer the sauce briskly until it thickens. Take **6 basil leaves,** roll them up lengthwise, and cut across the roll, slicing them very thinly. (You get the idea? This recipe, from the angel hair on up, is about skinny stuff.) Stir the basil into the sauce and add **1 sprig of fresh oregano.** Whisk in **1 ounce unsalted butter** and season to taste with **salt and pepper.** Now on to the pasta. Keeping the sauce warm, bring a large pot of salted water to a boil. Add **½ pound dried angel hair pasta** and cook according to the instructions on the package, or until al dente. When the pasta is about finished, bring the sauce up to almost a boil. Drain the pasta, reserving the water, and transfer immediately to the sauce, stirring the two together. Cook the sauce and pasta together for 1 minute, adding **2 ounces of reserved pasta water.** Divide the pasta into 2 equal portions, and then spoon the remaining sauce from the pan over the pasta and garnish with **Parmigiano cheese.** *Bon appétit!*

Julia is hardly the only mentor I've had in the restaurant business. I learned a similar lesson about giving yourself passionately to people from Wolfgang Puck. Years ago, I went to his restaurant Postrio in San Francisco and there he was, lighting up the room. A few nights later, I visited Spago, another of his restaurants in Los Angeles, and there he was again, talking to Billy Crystal. And then he came over and started talking to me! I thought to myself, *How does this guy do it?* A day or two after that, when I went to another restaurant of his in Santa

Monica, Chinois on Main—he's there! The guy must have had a twin or something. Keep in mind, he was world famous, a big star—he didn't need to work so hard anymore, but he did, and I took notice. I had only a few restaurants, but seeing how excited everyone was to talk to Wolfgang, I resolved to get to my restaurants as much as I possibly could, for the benefit of both the guests and our staff. At the time it wasn't natural for me to do that—I tended to be a bit shy, uncomfortable with the attention—but I realized I needed to get past it.

Bobby Hillson, owner of Seaside, also taught me a thing or two, especially after I was promoted to busser from my first post of pouring coffee and cutting desserts. The first Saturday we worked together, with him as manager, I ran around as fast as I could, eager to impress. A party of eight came in, and we had to push two tables together. Having never done it before, I forgot to remove the salt and pepper shakers and the flowers. They slid off and crashed onto the floor. I almost started to cry because I thought I was going to get fired. Bobby, who had been standing right there, came over and put his arm around me. "Steve, don't worry about it. Your attitude is unbelievable. You're going to make it in this business. Trust me, don't worry about it. Just relax and get a broom."

Nobody had ever given me a pep talk like that before in a restaurant. I learned right then how valuable they are, and it has made me a much better manager. I've probably given a thousand pep talks to people who have broken things in front of me—people with the same deer-in-the-headlights look I had that day. And like me, they were motivated to pick themselves up, feel better about themselves, and learn from their mistakes.

Mentors don't have to come from business; you can find them in your personal life, too. I've had so many mentors in my life—maybe ten or twenty of them. My dad taught me to pay attention and never stop learning, among many other things. Bill Rodan, my high school football coach, taught me to never quit and do the best I could every day. Steve Mindich, owner of the *Boston Phoenix* newspaper, taught me how to have a winning lunch business. Charlie Sarkis, owner of thirty-five restaurants, taught me about taking care of guests and team members. And my neighbor, Mr. Sampsonas, taught me that no matter how successful you are, you can't ever take your eye off your family.

We often think of mentors in a formal sense, as people who consciously take you under their wing and show you the way. Those I've mentioned didn't necessarily do that; rather, they're people to whom I simply looked for wisdom, people who knowingly or unknowingly influenced me in some way. Mentors don't proclaim whether they are mentors to us or not. *We* define who our mentors are. And the way we do that is simply by deciding to pay attention and learn from the people around us.

Take my cousin Mona. She is about fifteen years older than me and also my godmother. Her MO: She asks a lot of questions. She's a question maniac. When I was growing up, she drove me *crazy* with questions. She would ask about my life and my opinions about everything and anything. She was just so interested in what I thought. I noticed this, and I realized that this style of engaging people was perfect when you're interviewing them for a job. When we hire people at Davio's, the managers take a crack at the applicant first, and at the end I come in—*bam!*—asking all kinds of questions. Thanks to Mona, I have developed a knack for getting the real information out of people. Like how passionate they are. Whether they have out-of-control egos or not. Whether they're honest or not. Whether they're team players or not. And also, whether they're willing and eager to learn from others, or not.

The title of this chapter says it all: Pay attention, and you'll find that mentors are all around you. I can't emphasize that enough—I say it all the time to up-and-coming servers and bartenders. We've got to constantly observe what's happening around us. It may seem like nothing is going on, but really there are fifty interesting things happening that we can learn from at all times. The more we notice, the more we understand. It's up to us to appreciate the admirable people we cross paths with in life, observe what they do, and take them on in our minds and hearts as people who will influence us.

More broadly, it's up to us to make the most of the good business ideas that we come into contact with each and every day. In restaurants there is nothing new under the sun. Everybody borrows from everybody else. We can learn everything we need to succeed by receiving inspiration from what's already out there. I've already told you how I discovered the large-pot technique we once used to cook pasta. The idea of using little carafes to measure and pour wine by the glass I took from Mario Batali's restaurant Babbo in New York City. Do you have any idea how much money I have saved by pouring guests the same five-ounce serving each time, instead of the six or seven ounces our bartenders might pour by eyeball-ing it? Mario, I'll be sending you a check.

To this day, I eat out in other restaurants as often as I can just to see if I can learn something I don't already know. Whenever restaurants hand out paper menus, I take them. I am constantly watching food shows on TV and reading food magazines.

Sometimes you're lucky and people actually come to you with good ideas. In these situations it's important to be open-minded enough to listen. I know that sounds kind of obvious, but so many restaurateurs don't do it! Too bad, because they don't know what they're missing. Some of my most successful business ideas emerged out of great suggestions other people brought to me.

In 2002 I had a meeting with Tony Pangaro, our landlord at Arlington Street in Boston. We were talking about a little space that exists in the lobby of a building near our restau-rant. "Steve, I think you should use that as a take-out shop. Sell sandwiches and salads from Davio's. What do you think?" I wasn't too keen on the idea. We didn't focus on sandwiches and salads; it wasn't a core part of our brand. But I have a lot of respect for Tony, so I looked into it. At Balthazar in New York, I saw how a little cafe was connected to the restaurant, selling soups and salads. And I discovered a similar concept in a couple of other restaurants around the country. "You know," I said to myself, "maybe we can do that, too."

I put together a menu for the space to show Tony, and he loved it. "This is exactly what I had in mind. Go for it!" Today, we gross nearly $1 million a year in that little take-out shop, selling hundreds of fresh-made sandwiches and salads a day.

Spinach Salad

Remove the stems from **8 ounces baby spinach**, then wash, drain, and pat dry thoroughly. Place in a bowl. In a saucepan **mix 2 tablespoons extra virgin olive oil** (Monini preferred), a **pinch of garlic**, and **3 tablespoons balsamic vinegar** and cook over low heat until warm. Season with **small pinches of kosher salt and freshly ground black pepper.** Take your bowl filled with spinach and add to it **1 large, sliced portobello mushroom** and **2 ounces sliced roasted red peppers.** Grab your balsamic mixture and toss it all together. Portion out 4 servings in their own little bowls or plates. But wait: Don't forget to add **fresh goat cheese** to each dish and to serve (and eat!) as soon as possible. You don't want that warm dressing on the spinach to get cold.

It's insane! And I thank Tony for that. I never would have done it if it weren't for him. (And he reminds me every time he sees me. "So," he says, "how is my take-out shop doing?")

An even bigger success of ours came in 2006, when Jonathan Kraft, president of the New England Patriots football team, suggested that we package our spring rolls and sell them at retail to consumers and at wholesale to hotels and other restaurants. I really doubted whether this idea would fly; I knew that there were so many dimensions of that business I would need to figure out, such as production processes, marketing, getting USDA approval—everything. I was a restaurant guy; that's what I knew. Was it really smart to branch so far out? I'll talk more about brand extensions later, but for now let me just say that I thought about it for a while and researched it, simply because I respected how smart Jonathan was as a businessman (he's actually the smartest person

I know). Eventually, I decided to go for it. Today, our packaged Davio's products sell in three thousand stores around the country. They're a $10 million business and rapidly growing. All because I was willing to keep my ears open and listen.

~~

Although I strongly believe that mentors—defined as people from whom we can learn—are everywhere, I do think we all need one or more deeper relationships in our professional lives, people we can complain to and bounce ideas off of, and who do the same for us. Maybe these aren't mentors per se, but rather just good friends who provide a certain amount of coaching, camaraderie, and support.

One of my best friends is Herb Chambers, who owns about fifty car dealerships and has about two thousand team members in the New England area. Herb is unbelievable—a real inspiration. He's about nineteen years older than me and worth hundreds of millions of dollars. Other people in his position would have packed it in and hit the golf course for life. Yet Herb still has that fire. He *can't wait* to get to the office every day. Money doesn't drive him; the sheer pleasure of doing business does. He's texting me all the time about how many cars he sold on a given day, what the trends are. He's also holding "Coffee with Herb" events for people who buy his cars and helping to open new dealerships. He never takes his success for granted, and he's always still looking for ways to get ahead.

We can be anywhere and people will come up to Herb eager to tell him about the car they just bought from one of his dealerships. Other business owners might brush these people off, but not Herb. He'll spend five, ten minutes or even longer talking, excited to see these people as if he knows them personally. "Who was that guy?" I'll ask after we've walked away. "It's a customer," he'll say, "and I owe it all to them." What a lesson. If someone like Herb, at his level, can stay so dedicated to customers, then certainly I can, too.

Once we were in Europe at a store buying sneakers. Herb asked how much a pair cost, and the clerk said they were 300 euros but he could give Herb 20 percent off if he paid cash. Herb asked if I had some cash on me, but I didn't have enough, so he ran across the street to an ATM. He had probably spent about $50,000 in fuel to get us to Europe on his gulfstream jet, we were hanging out on a two-hundred-foot yacht he owns, and here he was, still looking to save 60 euros. It was another incredible lesson: Always stay hungry and go for the best deal. Never rest easy. You should never stop doing what it originally took to get you where you are.

If you ask Herb, I think he'll tell you that you're never too old for mentors. He looks to me as a mentor, even though I am younger than him. People who know us both will pull me aside and say, "Man, it's crazy. All Herb talks about is you and how much he learned from your spring roll business and the service at Davio's." At sales meetings Herb mentions how we treat our guests at Davio's and asks his team what they can do to serve their own customers even better. Jeff Davis, the general manager at one of Herb's Mercedes dealerships, poked fun at me, saying, "I'm so *sick* of hearing about Davio's at our meetings! Enough already." That means a lot. I have always looked up to Herb, and it is amazing to know that he respects what I do enough to want to learn from it.

Learning from mentors is a never-ending, lifelong practice. The more you learn and become successful, the more you naturally want to give back. That's why I'm writing this book. I remember what it was like as a student at Boston University when I was trying to get help from established businesses and people wouldn't take the time to return my calls. So let me end this chapter with an offer: If you're thinking about starting a business and want some more advice, give me a call. If I'm not busy mingling with guests, or spending time with my family, or figuring out how we can do an even better job than we already are, I'll be happy to share what I know. But basically what I know is this: Pay attention, take it all in, stay open-minded, try to improve. You can't go wrong.

Restaurant Lessons to Live By

Skip the arrogance. People starting a business need all the help they can get. None of us knows it all.

Mentors aren't just people who formally take us under their wings. We define who our mentors are simply by deciding to pay attention.

You don't need to reinvent the wheel. Immerse yourself in what others are already doing, and if something resonates, think about how you might adapt it.

When people come to you with ideas, keep an open mind. Even if the ideas seem crazy at first, they just might work.

You're never too old or too successful to have a mentor. You always have something to learn, something about your businesses you can improve.

CHAPTER FIVE

Treat Your People Like Family

Not a week goes by, it seems, when I don't get a request from my eighty-six-year-old dad that runs something like this: "Steve, I don't like to ask, but we're running short again. Your mother wants to know, do you think you can bring more meatballs by?"

My answer is always yes—not just because he's my dad and he loves our meatballs, but because when I make the delivery, I walk away with valuable business advice. On one recent occasion, he reminded me of something he's been saying for years. "The people, Steve. It's all about having good people. You can't get anywhere without them. And you have to treat them right. Then watch, they treat *you* right. I could tell you so many great stories. What a time I had."

I've always thought of my company like my extended family, and I've tried to create a warm workplace where everyone feels cared for. As an illustration, I'd like to introduce you to one of the most inspirational people I know, Patty LaBella. Not Patti LaBelle, the Grammy Award–winning singer. Patty LaBella, the sales manager at our Boston location.

Patty is an attractive woman in her mid-forties, with long brown hair and a nice smile. She does a great job serving our guests, helping them book exceptional dinners and other events in our private function rooms. She's funny, bubbly, and knows how to have a good time. She has many personal interests, including gardening, cooking, skiing, the beach, and entertaining. She especially loves Bruce Springsteen, something I discovered firsthand when I took her to a couple of concerts.

Life hasn't been easy for Patty. In 2002 her husband died, followed by her mother. For several years before she remarried, she had to raise her young son on her own. Then, in 2010, tragedy struck again when she was diagnosed with breast cancer. Thanks to our health care plan—available to all our staff working thirty hours or more a week—she received excellent care. She took a three-month leave of absence and returned with her cancer in check. Two years later, the cancer was back, this time in her bones. She got a hip replacement, missing another three months of work.

Today, she's undergoing chemo to fight new tumors that have popped up along her spine. Given all that Patty has been through, I'd understand if she showed up at work depressed and projecting a "woe is me" attitude. She doesn't. Every day she's her normal cheerful self, entertaining us and laughing with guests on the phone. When I ask how she does it, working so hard for us and handling trivial requests for a certain kind of sparkling water, all the while dealing with her terrible diagnosis, she says, "What choice do I have? You just have to keep going. You can't let it get you down."

Occasionally, when I'm talking to Patty one-on-one, she'll let go and cry. The pain just sneaks up on her. But man, she is one tough lady—and a great supporter of Davio's. Recognizing how much Patty has done for our company, how much she has inspired us and served our guests, I make sure we go the extra mile for her. Each time she was on leave, we kept paying her full salary. We didn't have to do that, but we knew she had a mortgage and other responsibilities, and we wanted to help. We're talking six months of a professional salary over a two-year period. We also cut her in on the bonuses our sales staff receives as a percentage of sales. Did her colleagues complain? On the contrary, they pitched in, picking up portions of her duties so we didn't have to hire a replacement for Patty.

I can't tell you how many times we've paid full salaries to people who were out sick, nor can I recall how many small loans I personally have made to people in need. If you want to win in this business or in any business, you can't just *talk* about treating people right; you have to deliver. Our team members stay with us for decades and are unusually committed to our success because they *know* our company will help them during their time in need. But it's more than that. People love to work for us because on a daily basis we show them the same level of respect and care we show our paying guests. Treat people like family, as my father always did, and you wind up with a thriving business filled with motivated, dedicated, respectful individuals. People like Patty LaBella.

⌒

I didn't merely have my father telling me to treat people right when I was a kid; I saw it happening myself in the company he helped run. Before my dad retired he was president of

UniFirst, an industrial uniform supply company. It started as our family business with a single plant; today it is a publicly traded, billion-dollar global company, with my cousin Ronny serving as chairman and president, my cousin Cindy as treasurer, my brother Dave as vice president, and my brother-in-law Mike as head of national accounts. Growing up, I worked at the company during the summer and on vacations, and I could see how generous management was with the team members. The company provided not only a good salary and benefits, but extras like profit sharing. It paid off: While the industrial uniform business was heavily unionized, with the usual share of labor tensions, UniFirst was much more harmonious and eventually even became a nonunion shop. The loyalty of longtime team members also helped fuel the company's explosive growth.

Later in life, I came to see that the opposite principle held true—that treating team members poorly could send a company downhill. Every six weeks for about fifteen years, I went to this guy Spencer to get my hair cut. He was that good. But I quickly noticed something funny: I would never get the same person washing my hair twice. *Never.* They just came and went. Several years into it, I started thinking to myself, "Is this the time I'll get a repeat hair washer?" But it never happened! Spencer was clearly very difficult to work for. He was rude and obnoxious and didn't hesitate to ream his people out in front of his guests. The young shampooers he hired couldn't stand it, so they kept leaving. I told myself that I never, ever wanted to run a business like that. It's expensive to train new people to do their jobs well, and I wanted to give those who worked with me the incentive to stick around. I thought it would be way more fun and less stressful to run a company where people *wanted* to spend time.

Bad behavior on the job is hardly limited to barbershops. When I was seventeen I got my first job as a doorman at Frankenstein's, a club that used to show old movies. The owners opened a new place called Play It Again, Sam's, and when I turned eighteen I went to work there as a bartender. Thursday night was ladies' night from 7:30 to 9:00 p.m.—just me, two other guys bartending, and dozens of women throwing money around. I learned a lot then about sexuality, and I was making $250 to $300 working just one night a week. Unfortunately, the manager, Boris, was a real jerk who fired people for no reason.

One night, I was in there off duty, drinking beer and watching movies with my girlfriend, when Boris came up to me. "Steve, I just fired someone. I can't look at this guy anymore, and I need someone at the bar. How about you go take over?"

"Boris," I said, "are you kidding me? I have the night off. I've been drinking. I can't bartend like that. I'll make a mistake and hurt someone—or worse, myself. I could cut myself slicing limes. Who knows what could happen."

"Steve, come on, I need you to do this."

"I can't. I'm sorry. You know I would do anything for you. I just can't right now. I've probably had five or six beers."

He crossed his arms and shot me a stern look. "Steve, if you don't get behind the bar right now, I'm gonna fire you, too."

"Really?" I said. "You're gonna fire me because I've been drinking and don't want to work because of that?"

He nodded. "Yeah."

I threw up my hands. "Okay, you don't have to fire me. We'll just leave." And that was it. I never worked there again. Instead, I went to work at Seaside as a coffee clerk making maybe $30 a night instead of $300. I liked it much better, but even there some people in charge didn't treat others well. One bartender named Micky was crazy and would yell at you when you got something wrong. You had to place your guests' bar requests in a precise order—vodka drinks first, then gin, then draft beers. If you didn't, he would literally walk away. It was ridiculous! I worked in fear of the guy and couldn't wait for my shift to end. Micky wound up getting fired when a guest with a scar on her face asked for coffee, and he responded, "Hey, Scarface, what do you think this is, a fucking coffee shop?"

Today, I see the same thing all the time on reality TV shows: chefs and other bosses who rant and rave and terrorize their colleagues. All this is unnecessary and bad business practice. Show me a well-run restaurant, and I'll show you a place that's way too boring for television. It's a place where people care about each other and help each other out. It's also a place where people might not get it right every time, but where they do their best to learn from their mistakes.

⌐—

A big reason I've tried to treat people like family is that I want them to work well together as a team. Most businesses depend on teams, but in restaurants they're absolutely critical. Each meal we serve goes through at least ten sets of hands, from the person who receives our supplies, to the prep cooks who clean, cut, and prepare the ingredients, to the line chefs, the food runners, and the servers. Each of these people matters. One weak link, one person distracted and not doing his or her job, and we're in for a rough ride. Let's say the place is packed, and the food runner—the person who brings the food from the kitchen to the table—presents the wrong dishes to each guest at a table of eight. The guests cut into their steaks and then realize they weren't what they ordered. Everything has to be sent back and made again—for an entire table—which causes the kitchen to get backed up, affecting other tables. The complaints pile in, and we wind up looking bad. All because one food runner made a small mistake. This scenario might sound unlikely, but trust me, it happens all the time in restaurants.

One of the most embarrassing days of my career involved a breakdown in teamwork, albeit one that I helped create. It occurred just after we had moved from our original Boston location to a much larger space. We were booked weeks out for dinner, but our private function rooms weren't seeing enough party business yet, so I decided to open them up to a la carte dining, too. Big mistake.

Our team wasn't designed to handle the extra volume. We needed two guys on the grill and two making pasta, but we had only one of each. We didn't have a chef expeditor, someone who's job it is to organize the various components of an order as it is being assembled; nor did we have enough food runners to bring food to guests when it was hot and ready. As a result, the chefs—who were already slammed with orders—were taking time to organize the food as it was coming out. We made mistakes, food was delayed, and many guests were very, very unhappy. Some waited two hours before walking out. They insulted me by saying things like, "You should go back to Newbury Street!" and "You have no idea what you're doing!" and "This restaurant is too big!" and "You're not that good anyway!" I'm sure some of these people never came back.

The next day, the chefs and I spent hours completely redesigning our system, ensuring that something like this would never happen again. Fortunately, it hasn't. But even with the right system in place, as we now have, and competent people who understand their jobs, you still need a strong spirit of teamwork, or you're screwed. You're only as good as your last meal. You can lose your clientele almost overnight. You cannot afford to mess up, not even a little, so you can't have people just looking out for themselves. They have to *care* about the restaurant, their colleagues, and the guests enough to do their very best every minute. They have to take pride in their work. And they have to be happy on the job. But all this means that they have to feel valued, respected, and embraced as members of a company's extended family.

How do you create the feeling of an extended family? What do you actually have to do, besides helping your employees out when they're in trouble? Let's start by not calling them *employees.* That word stinks. Scour previous pages of this book—I defy you to see a single instance when I used that word. You won't see me using a word like *customer,* either. It's okay for companies in other industries to speak of *customers,* but in the hospitality industry, expectations are different.

I use *guest* instead of *customer,* and I have a really cool substitute for *employee,* too. I learned it while taking a class with Jackie Sonnabend, Executive Vice President and Senior Quality Officer for Sonesta International Hotels. She blew me away with the idea that everyone in a workplace—including the owner—should treat colleagues as well as they do paying guests. It's obvious (or should be) the kind of service a guest should receive from a server, a bartender, or a hostess. Our own people—our "inner guests," as Sonnabend so memorably called them—should get the same courtesy, respect, and kindness. If we all treat each other well, as inner guests, this will naturally incline us to provide superior service to "outer guests," too.

We're using the word *guest* when talking about restaurants because restaurants are places of hospitality. You're welcoming someone in who doesn't normally belong there, like you would a guest to your own home. What the term *inner guest* conveys is the idea that we should do the same for people who *work* at a restaurant. As my dad emphasized, the same basic principle holds true—or should hold true—at any business, whether or not we normally think of it as a hospitality business.

Inner guest implies a clear standard of behavior on the part of managers and others in charge, as well. No shouting. No throwing pots and pans. No berating people when they screw up. No arguing. No rude or sarcastic comments. No ordering people around. Would you treat a daughter or son in these ways? I sure hope not. And since people in charge aren't allowed to act like jerks on the job, *nobody* is. Ettore, the Philadelphia Davio's general manager, fired a server because he was treating a busser like his slave. Ettore sat the guy down and asked him to stop, but the behavior continued. The server thought he was superior to the busser. "Listen," Ettore told him, "do Steve and I act like that to you? Steve's the owner of the company, and I'm your superior. We don't do that. So you can't, either." He didn't listen, so he was gone.

If you've spent any time around restaurants, you're probably thinking I'm out of touch. Restaurants have a reputation for being raw, high-pressure places where the f-bombs fly. Not my restaurants. A reality TV producer would hate Davio's because he wouldn't hear many bleeps in our back of house. Would you say "fuck you" to a guest? We don't allow our people to say it to each other—even when our paying guests aren't around. It's incredible what a difference this makes. The whole tenor of the restaurant changes. A standard of respect is set. Do you remember how Mayor Giuliani cut down on major crimes in New York City by enforcing laws against petty crimes like spraying graffiti or peeing in public? It's like that for us. Ban the f-bombs, and over time, the staff just gets along better, helps each other, even *likes* each other—and treats paying guests better.

But the idea of the "inner guest" takes us beyond basic civility. There's an old saying that a family that eats together stays together. Restaurants obviously feed their paying guests, but I think they should feed their inner guests, too. We hold staff meals at 11:00 a.m. and 4:15 p.m. every day, free of charge. Everybody comes: the chefs, the front of the house, and me if I'm around. We talk, joke around, and have a great time. The food is so plentiful and good that if you work for us full time, you don't have to go to the supermarket very often; you have a pretty comprehensive Davio's meal plan at your disposal. People joke about the "Davio's ten"—the ten pounds you gain upon first coming to work with us. Does this cost us money? Sure, but we benefit, too. It's a lot easier for our people to team up with their colleagues and serve guests well when they're socializing with their colleagues before every shift.

We extend this treatment to other people we do business with. You know that guy who delivers fruits and vegetables? He gets a sandwich and a soda. We benefit because the next time he's taking a box of romaine lettuce out for us, and he knows that one box is better than another, he'll probably give us the good box. The guys who valet our guests' cars get fed. I see *no* other restaurants doing that, and I don't get it. The valets are the first people a guest sees when she gets out of her car. Sometimes guests will ask a valet, "Hey, the food here—is it good?" I want the valet to love Davio's so much that he opens the door with a big smile and says, "Welcome to Davio's. The meatballs rock and the spring roll appetizers are *awesome.*"

When I talk about feeding people, I'm not suggesting that as the owner you should socialize with team members generally. In fact, I strongly suggest you *don't* go out drinking after hours with team members or attend parties at their houses. I've taken personal days only a couple of times over the last thirty years. One was when my golden retriever Maggie died; I was just too upset to face people the next day. The other was when Tania, a general manager at the time, asked if I wanted to grab a drink after work. "Sure," I said, "let's go have a drink." I didn't realize that she went to Penn State and was a huge party queen. I got totally wasted that night and was sick at home for two days, the bathroom floor my best friend. I haven't had tequila since. Even the smell of it makes me dizzy.

Today's sexual harassment laws make it dicier to have fun like that. More important, it's hard to go out for beers with someone and the next day sit him down and tell him he's not doing a good job. Just like parents today are sometimes too much of a pal to their kids, I think restaurant owners often fail to keep a healthy distance. When I was growing up, we called parents Mr. Imbrescia, Mrs. Deluca, Mr. Sampsonas. We didn't call them Sal or John. As a boss you need to keep some basic sense of decorum and authority. I take my managers out socially because I think it's helpful to have an "inner circle" at my company. I need managers to be my eyes and ears, and I want us to build up trust with one another. But that's as far as I go in building friendships with my team members.

Another huge thing we do at some of our locations to bring the "inner guest" idea to life is pool our tips. At most restaurants servers get tips only from tables they handle. But our servers give all their tip money to one or two of their peers to divide up equally. This can work two ways: Some nights, you work slow tables and make more from the shared pool than you'd otherwise earn. Other nights, you work an extravagant party that tips lavishly, and make less. At other restaurants, when servers get tip money only from the tables they work, they wind up looking out for their own three or four tables, and they don't think much about helping anybody else. Have you ever walked into a restaurant and seen one server running around and sweating while off in a corner two other servers are chatting? It drives me crazy! I feel like shaking these other two and saying, "What the hell are you doing? Can't you see this guy? Can you bus his table? Get some water for his guests? Deliver his food?"

In a family people naturally help each other out without even being asked. Staff at a good restaurant delivers similar treatment to every guest: We don't wait for guests to ask us to pull their chairs out for them or re-fold their napkins; we do it automatically. Team members should behave in this considerate, thoughtful way toward the *inner* guest, and if you pool tips, they do. At our restaurants team members rush to help each other if something breaks, because they're not tied to their stations; they don't have to worry about getting a lower tip (and in any case, someone else is thinking the same thing and covering their table, too). When a table's food is ready to be served, a whole team can deliver it at once, fill all the wine glasses, and clear away all the appetizer plates—because each team member isn't worried only about her tables. Pooled tips also help us avoid other pitfalls that comes from selfishness, such as the bickering you see in many places over how many tables each person gets, or the tendency of servers to push an extra dessert or glass of wine just to get their own personal guest average up.

Some servers can't handle pooled tips. They use it as an excuse to slack off. "You know what?" they say. "Why not take my time on my last table? I'm still going to make the same amount." Or they resent making a little less than they would if they were working the same tables at another restaurant. If servers are thinking only about themselves, then they're not Davio's people. It has to be about *us*. And if servers are only about right now, then they're also not Davio's people. Servers have to be about tomorrow, next week, next month, next year. Today, they might make less than they would elsewhere, but over the long term, they'll do pretty darn well (some of my servers drive Mercedes and own homes and investment properties). And they'll be treated much better in so many other ways than at the restaurant down the street. They'll be treated like family.

—✒

I could talk all day long about the inner guest. It's that important to me. What's also important is the heavy responsibility that owners of a business have. Banning swearing and other bad behavior feels uninspiring or even false when the owner isn't taking care of team members in all kinds of other ways. I give not only health insurance to my inner guests but also dental and life. I've been doing this for twenty-eight years—since Day One. When a good team member has trouble with alcohol or drugs, I don't just fire them; I first try to work with them and get them into some kind of treatment program. And everybody, from the dishwasher on up, gets paid vacations. After a year you get a week off annually; after three years you get two weeks, and it goes up from there. We have some guys who get five weeks off every year because they've been with us for twenty-five years.

Just as important is being willing to listen to issues people have when they arise, and to take a personal stake in resolving them. Everyone at Davio's has my e-mail address and knows that I read what they send and I respond. I rotate through our restaurants every week, sitting down with staff at all levels to see how things are going. I don't care how successful you get as a businessperson—you have to keep talking to people face-to-face, because otherwise they start thinking that you don't care, that what you say about the company being a family is just words.

Most strong families have a peacemaker in them, which is why owners should take it upon themselves to personally resolve disputes that arise between team members. In 2003 two longtime servers, Tonino and Alan, weren't getting along. Tonino had been with Davio's from the beginning, and Alan had gone to college with me and worked with me at Seaside. The two hadn't talked in six months. I called them into a private function room and asked them what the deal was. "Oh, nothing," they said. "We're fine."

"When was the last time you talked to one another?"

No answer.

I laid down the law. "Guys, look, we've been friends over twenty years. We're not leaving this room until we work this thing out. So go ahead, sit down."

They sat down but still didn't say anything.

"I'm serious," I said. "I don't have anything to do. You guys don't want to talk, I'll sit here all day. Call your wife, Tonino, and tell her you'll be late. We're not leaving."

It was then that Tonino pointed at Alan and said, "He's an asshole!"

"Okay," I said, "we're getting somewhere, but that's the last time you're going to swear. If you're mad about something, we can talk reasonably."

Tonino grew red in the face. "Alan doesn't defend Davio's, Steve. He always complains. It's not right."

We had recently opened our expanded restaurant in Boston and were still working out the kinks (which, as you've read, were pretty major). Apparently, Alan hadn't raised issues he'd had with the manager on duty, but instead had vented his frustrations behind people's backs. This angered Tonino, who responded by doing some dumb things Alan didn't like. We were in that room for about two and a half hours, but we eventually worked it all out. Alan's concerns turned out to be

Sautéed Tonino Spinach

Over medium heat in a 10-inch sauté pan, sauté **½ teaspoon minced shallots** in **1½ tablespoons extra virgin olive oil** (Monini preferred). Add **1½ tablespoons golden raisins** and cook for about 1 minute. Mix in **1½ tablespoons pine nuts.** Increase the heat to high. Stir this mixture with a wooden spoon to scrape up the browned bits that cling to the bottom of the pan. Add **1 tablespoon butter** and allow it to melt before adding **5 cups packed baby spinach.** Stir or toss everything together with tongs until the spinach is wilted. Season with **salt and freshly ground pepper—** or don't add any!

valid; he just hadn't voiced them in the proper way. Tonino understood, and he and Alan got along well again. Both of them realized just how much I cared about their happiness and well-being on the job. Others in the company saw how I had dealt with their dispute and realized that, too.

I'm not suggesting that I personally handle every single dispute. I'd rather have a manager mediate between two bussers so that the manager's authority and power is felt. In the early days I made the mistake of interfering too much, and I found that the team didn't respect our managers; they only respected me. How does that make the manager feel about her job? And what does that say about how much trust I have in her competence?

Delegating responsibility to managers is in itself an important way to show caring and respect for your team. So is encouraging managers to do the same down the line. Giving everyone a chance to step up and be responsible does so much to help them feel valued. People want to be treated like adults. They want to feel competent. They want to make decisions. In a restaurant, there are many ways to make this happen. Tell people how much things cost, so that they can understand on their own why it's important not to waste or break them. Train people well, so they have the tools and knowledge they need to feel like they're excelling at their jobs. Don't let people call in sick to a manager; make them feel responsible for calling around and finding someone else to take their shift. When guests have a special request for the chef, empower servers to provide an answer without going to the kitchen to check. Empower them, too, to handle guest complaints without the manager's interference. At Davio's only managers can take a food item off the bill, but short of that, our servers have full authority to make amends, for instance by offering a free dessert or new entree.

Finally, hire well and promote from within. Don't let just anybody into the company; respect your people enough to put time and energy into getting the *right* people. Beyond looking for skills, I try to hire people who are team players and who see restaurant work like I do, as a calling, as God's work (and yes, I do take it that seriously). A guy who's worked at twenty-two places in three years is probably not a team player—and he's probably going to make the rest of our people miserable. But a guy who's done a lot of charity work? Chances are he'll be a great team player, because he's someone who really cares about other people. Once someone's on board, I give them a chance to rise up and make something of themselves. Seaside gave me a place to grow—from coffee clerk to busser to server to salad guy to sauté guy to head chef. Now I'm doing something similar, promoting my servers into management positions, and general managers into regional managers. The great thing about it for me is the chance to work with people like Patty LaBella for years and develop great bonds. Over time these people aren't just *like* family. They *are* family.

⌒

On our job applications we give people a list of things that a workplace can provide—money, respectful treatment, community, and so on—and ask them to rank the items according to their importance. Most people put money pretty far down the list. What matters to people is how they're treated. I know it matters to me. Even after I left Seaside, I came back and worked one night a week, or when they needed me. I toyed with keeping the job even after I started Davio's. I just liked being there. I liked the camaraderie, just like a football or hockey player likes being in the locker room and hanging with his teammates. What made the job for me wasn't the work, but the friendships.

If you have a job, I hope you feel this way about the place where you work. If you're thinking of starting a business, I hope you'll create a new place where people can feel this way. You can't run a business by yourself. Treating your people like family might cost a little more. It might take more of your time. But trust me, magic will happen. People won't steal from you. They'll pitch in when you need them to take an extra shift. They'll work hard to excel at their jobs. They'll stick with you through the hard times. They'll lend each other money when the need arises and help each other haul furniture when they're moving. They'll celebrate holidays together. And before you know it, you'll look back on your successful business and think, like my dad does, *What a wonderful ride it's been.*

Restaurant Lessons to Live By

Don't be a jerk to your team members. Otherwise, they just might leave in less than the time it takes to need another haircut.

If your workplace could be a reality TV show, then friend, you're doing something wrong.

Don't hire employees. Hire "inner guests."

A company that eats together stays together.

Creating a warm workplace rests ultimately on the owner's shoulders. Don't screw it up. But don't think you have to do everything. Delegate.

CHAPTER SIX

Keep Your Eye on the Money

Remember back in chapter one when I told you I had wanted to own a restaurant ever since I was a kid eating lobster tails at my cousin's wedding? Well, there was actually another occasion when I *really* knew.

I was nineteen years old, a sophomore at Boston University, and working at Seaside. I was in the kitchen late one night when a gorgeous server named Maria sailed in. She was topless except for whipped cream she'd arranged to cover her nipples. She shook her boobs at me, causing the white stuff to fly all over and hit me in the face. "What do you think of my Halloween costume, Steve?"

I thought it was pretty amazing that she even knew my name. I wiped my face and licked whipped cream off my finger. "I, uh, I love your costume," I said. And I did. It was a truly great Halloween costume.

"Cool," she said as she waltzed away.

"You know," I said to myself, "I really do have a future in this business."

Maria and I wound up going out drinking after our shift. Let's just say that my sexual education was enhanced that evening—and not just with whipped cream. When I woke up the next morning with Maria, who was even hotter with her uniform off, I thought once again, *This is awesome!*

Not long after, I was going over our inventory with the chef, Ricky Gordon, when I thought about this incident. In a flash it hit me how we could save a little money on our food costs. "Hey," I said, "we should make our whipped cream rather than use the canisters."

"Why is that, Steve?"

"Because there's never any gas in the cans. People go in there and suck on them to get high. We wind up throwing the cans out. If we make our own whipped cream, we can cut down on waste."

"Okay, great idea."

My point is this: Although those breasts burned themselves into my retinas, my eyes have always been on the money. As a kid I dreamed of being more successful than my father, just as he had outdid my grandfather. I grew up with a comfortable, upper-middle-class lifestyle, with a nice house and a pool, and I always wanted to have something similar for myself. Looking around at the restaurateurs on my street, I realized that they all had pretty nice lifestyles, too. *Geez,* I thought, *this restaurant thing might make sense. If I do a good job and take care of people, I could make some good money someday.* I was never interested *just* in making money, but in my mind money has always been part of the endgame of owning a restaurant.

If you have any hope of succeeding in business, whether a restaurant or anything else, you've got to pay attention to financial performance—all day, every day. This may sound obvious, but it's incredible how many restaurateurs don't do it. Maybe they're food guys who aren't so interested in numbers. Or they've had a good run for the first six months or a year and have gotten lazy. Whatever the case, they often wind up in trouble. You can have the best food in the world, but you're still a business, and a business is about making money. If you want to thrive for decades, not just a year or two, you've got to get real about the dollars and cents when you first open and *stay real* over time, paying special attention to your food costs, rent, labor, and sales. You can never let up. Not even when a topless server flings whipped cream in your face.

I've shared a lot of stories so far, but in this chapter I'd like to focus more on some important tricks of the trade. You prima donna chefs out there who don't have the time or patience to care about money should skip to the next chapter. For the rest of you, let's talk about starting up your restaurant. You've dreamed about it for so long—your own place. And now you're finally doing it. So here's a piece of wisdom: Don't screw it up by undercapitalizing!

Not having enough backing is the number one reason restaurants go under. You should start by figuring out how much it's going to cost to do your build out. Draw up a realistic budget. It costs us about $300 a square foot to build a restaurant. Sometimes you can build restaurants for $200 or $250 a square foot, but as I write this, $300 is a pretty good number in my big-city market. Still, don't stop there. Be sure to add an extra 25 percent on top of that to cover all kinds of unplanned expenditures. I can't emphasize how important that is.

During that first year you're probably not going to make money right away. It will take you six weeks to hire and train the staff. You might need more chairs, plates, silverware, and pots and pans than you initially think, or maybe you'll wind up having to redo some plumbing or wiring in the kitchen that you didn't anticipate or fix a machine you didn't know was broken. I've been doing this a long time, and I still can't estimate exactly everything I'm going to need. I don't want to have a gun to my head, worrying about money all the time. Who needs that stress? I want to be able to give my guests more value at the beginning, like offering larger portions or more reasonable prices. I want to do promotions, give away freebies to food writers and others in the media. All that costs money, so it's important not to feel strapped for cash because of unanticipated expenses.

One way to help yourself through your first six months to a year is doing what I did and getting a good lease. These days, I try to get up to six months of free rent from the day I open up a space. Even if you're sufficiently capitalized, the money you save allows you to really do the opening right, so that you stand a stronger chance of sticking around. Maybe you spend more on marketing, maybe you hire a couple extra staff members or make the portions larger. The landlord has to understand that the first year is critical to a restaurant's success. You need those rave reviews to establish your brand in a market. You also need to put forth your very best service, since many guests will give you only one try, maybe two. Blow that, my friend, and you're cooked. Most landlords I've dealt with get this and will do something to help restaurateurs get their feet on the ground. It's in their interests, too, to have you as a long-term tenant.

When I first opened Davio's, I underestimated the capital I would need, and it was tough. As I've related, that little restaurant I bought all those years ago had a ton of financial issues, including obligations to the IRS, to vendors, and to financial institutions. Now these were all *my* problems, because I bought the restaurant's assets and thus assumed its debts, too. Why would I buy such a problem-ridden place? Because the old owners had a fantastic, below-market lease that I thought I could profit from (and that I did eventually profit from). With that lease in hand, I started with $500,000, cobbled together from family, bank loans, and proceeds from the sale of two condominiums my father and I had purchased together. I wish I had had $750,000, because I was *way* under at first. What saved me was the extra $25,000 to $30,000 a week in sales we brought in once we changed the upstairs from a bar to a cafe. That was like found money to me, since running the cafe cost us comparatively little in addition to our existing expenses. I wound up paying all my debts as quickly as I could and saved an additional $300,000 to $400,000, which I used two years later to open my second location in the Boston suburb of Brookline.

As important as it is to have enough start-up capital, make sure you don't go too far in getting it. Never, *ever* put your own name on any loans you take out for your business. Why? Because if your business goes down, the bank is going to take your house. If you can't open without putting your house up, then you probably aren't ready to start a restaurant. Save more money, get a second job, take on some investors. I've seen talented chefs risk their homes, and then when things don't work out, they are so desperate for additional financing that they make terrible, painful deals with investors in order to survive. You don't want to go there. Know when to get into a business venture, but equally important, know when *not* to get in.

With enough capital in place, you have to make sure you have a good business model. That means having realistic sales goals, as well as a plan for the costs you'll be running. The big three costs you need to worry about are food, liquor, and labor. I advise trying to keep your food costs between 25 and 32 percent of food sales. The exact number will vary depending on what kind of restaurant you are; higher-end places will have higher food costs due to the higher-quality products they need to use. Liquor costs should be in the high teens to mid-twenties as a percentage of beverage sales, while all your labor costs combined should be around 25 percent of total sales. That should leave you with a profit of 5 to 15 percent. Obviously 15 percent is better, but with 5 you're at least getting by.

The biggest cost of all is food, so you should pay special attention to that. Cost your menu carefully before you open. Break down the dishes component by component—how much the chicken breast costs, the fresh herbs, the imported Parmigiano you use in the risotto. Some chefs put extremely expensive ingredients on their menu, not realizing that most people don't even know what that ingredient is. Many restaurants cost their regular menus properly, but not their specials. They just don't think the specials are all that big of a deal. Yet they are. You'll sell a lot of specials, and you don't want to let those push your overall food costs into the danger zone. *I can't emphasize enough how critical it is to cost your food.*

Davio's Penne Smoked Chicken
(with Cost Breakdown)

Begin by bringing a large pot of lightly salted water to a rolling boil. Cook **12 ounces penne pasta** uncovered, stirring occasionally, until the pasta has cooked through but is still firm to the bite, about 11 minutes. Drain it and set it aside for few minutes until the sauce is done. In a large skillet over medium-high heat, add **2 ounces butter**, **12 ounces heavy cream**, and **2 ounces rehydrated and chopped sun-dried tomatoes.** After about 3 minutes, when the liquid begins to reduce, add **2 ounces whole walnuts**, **2 ounces chopped scallions, 8 ounces smoked chicken chopped into 1-inch cubes,** and **4 ounces grated Parmigiano-Reggiano cheese,** stirring occasionally. When the chicken seems heated through and the heavy cream has reduced by half, the sauce should be done. Gently fold the pasta into the chicken mixture. Add **2 ounces pasta water** and stir thoroughly. Season with **salt and pepper.** You'll have enough for two portions.

Cost breakdown (per portion):

Penne pasta:	$0.53
Butter:	$0.11
Heavy cream:	$0.56
Sun-dried tomatoes:	$0.15
Walnuts:	$0.38
Scallions:	$0.37
Smoked chicken:	$1.40
Cheese:	$0.56
Salt, Pepper:	$0.08
Total cost per portion:	$4.14
Retail price of dish:	$22.00

Food cost as percentage of selling price: 18.8 percent (well below our upper limit of 32 percent)

Your food costs could be up at 50 percent, and you won't know it for thirty or forty-five days, until you get the bills from your suppliers. By then it's too late—you'll have been losing money every day just by being open! It will almost be cheaper to *close* than to keep selling your food with screwed-up costs.

It might seem like I'm overly obsessive about costs. There's a reason: I got burned. When I opened our second Davio's in Brookline, I had a five-thousand-square-foot space that was bringing in $2.5 million in sales, which was great for the time. We were busy every night. Yet we had a mortgage on the building our restaurant was in, and it was very expensive. We really needed to be bringing in $3.5 million in sales to make a nice profit.

We couldn't do that, though, because we couldn't charge the same prices in Brookline that we did in Boston—the market just wouldn't support it. A $20 Boston dish would get us only $14 in Brookline. Yet our food and liquor costs were the same. You see our problem: We hadn't costed the menu properly. We hadn't figured out what our costs needed to be in order to make the margin we needed to survive. Our food costs were almost 40 percent of sales, when they needed to be in the high 20s. Since we couldn't scrimp on quality without damaging our brand, we were stuck with our costs, and we eventually had to sell the building and leave Brookline—despite being busy every night.

~~

Let's say that you have enough money to start with and a plan to turn a profit each month, and that your business plan is working. You make it through the initial six to twelve months.

You're not going anywhere. What then? How do you stay in business? As I've suggested, it's a question not enough businesspeople ask. They're so flush with their initial success that they think they can just leave the business on cruise control and move on to the next thing. Or even worse, hang out at the bar getting drunk with the guests. Whoo, boy. It's like they're just *willing* themselves into poverty and an early grave.

You can *never* take your eye off the money—and specifically, the costs you're running. It's tempting to let the little things go, like not caring how much wine you pour into a glass. But if you're overpouring a glass by an ounce each time, that's going to add up over hundreds or thousands of pours. An ounce is a huge thing! Likewise, it might not seem such a big deal to have an extra cook in the kitchen. But it is. Over time that unneeded set of hands is going to boost your labor costs. What we do at Davio's is try to keep our hourly labor costs in the kitchen at less than 10 percent of food sales, opting when we can for cheaper, less experienced labor. I'd rather have two $12-an-hour guys than one $24-an-hour guy. I can always take the cheaper people under my wing and train them to work the way *I* want them to, and I've got two bodies to help, not just one.

What about salaried labor? Many restaurateurs fall into the trap of hiring too many salaried managers as they grow. They add layer upon layer of expensive bureaucracy to their operations—largely out of arrogance. You see these guys with two or three restaurants who have a regional manager, a corporate chef, a VP of human resources, and on and on. I feel like saying: dude, you've got two freakin' restaurants—big deal!

Keep your management structure as flat as possible. When I had four restaurants, I still kind of served as corporate chef and corporate manager. Realizing I was spread too thin, I promoted Ettore, the general manager of our Philadelphia location, and gave him the additional title and responsibilities of director of operations. When I opened a fifth restaurant, I appointed Rodney, one of our chefs, as corporate chef but had him continue his duties at his original restaurant. I also put Paul Flaherty in charge of two new Davio's locations in addition to his main restaurant in Foxboro, Massachusetts. I could have hired new people for these bigger jobs, but it is more cost effective and strategically sound to keep my senior managers rooted in specific locations. That way, they don't develop a "corporate headquarters" mentality and lose track of day-to-day operations.

For food costs here's another trick: Screen your vendors carefully and stick with the good ones. We're a member of an organization called Dining Alliance, a group of independent restaurants that cooperatively buy from common vendors to get the best value. Over the last five years, while food prices in America have gone up, the prices we pay have gone down. This allows us to continue to give our guests the highest quality ingredients without raising our prices.

As a member of Dining Alliance, we work only with top-end vendors like Foley Fish, Cambridge Packing, and Fazenda Coffee, and even then we constantly check them. We weigh our steaks and fish to make sure that when we order fifty pounds, we get fifty pounds. We don't hesitate to call up our vendors when something's not right. We're known around town as a tough customer, which is exactly the way we want it. We want to keep our vendors on their toes, so they give us the very best quality for the money and don't overcharge us. Don't hesitate to visit your vendor's warehouses or production facilities. That way, they'll know how attentive you are, and they'll feel motivated to go above and beyond.

To really monitor costs, don't just do it occasionally—make it a regular practice, and involve members of your team. The chart on page 101 shows just one part of the monthly statement we created recently for one of our restaurants.

You can see how closely we break things down—meat, seafood, produce, etc. We can look at how much one category cost us as a percentage of total cost, and in our full monthly statement, we compare present costs to historic cost figures. Why is seafood a greater percentage of our cost than it was a year or two ago? How does it compare to produce? Are they both in the desired range? Are there things we can do to pare these costs without affecting quality? We ask similar questions for our labor and general operating costs, too.

Big monthly statements are great, but if you wait for the end of the month, you've waited too long. I'm constantly hammering my managers with questions about food, beverage, and labor. Our chefs sit down every day with the numbers and costs clearly broken down by category. And they know that I'm *always* interested in the numbers. I keep my handy little smartphone with me everywhere I go, checking it at odd hours of the day or night—like at 3:00 a.m. when I get up to go to the bathroom. If anyone e-mails me with money updates or questions, they're shocked to get a response in the middle of the night. In truth, I just happened to be up, but they don't know that. They think I'm up late working, calculating our costs and how we can better control them. (Meanwhile, my wife thinks I have an intestinal problem because I'm in the bathroom so long texting or e-mailing numbers with our team.)

Monthly Statement

Cost of Goods Sold

5000 • Meat cost	$19,217.35	8.40%
5002 • Seafood cost	$17,307.17	7.57%
5004 • Produce cost	$12,576.55	5.50%
5005 • Dairy cost	$7,305.42	3.19%
5007 • Kitchen alcohol cost	$457.46	0.20%
5008 • Coffee cost	$1,101.88	0.48%
5009 • Dry/baked goods cost	$13,003.99	5.69%
5010 • Freight – food	$1,786.84	0.78%
5013-01 • Food Inventory Change	$1,877.17	0.82%
5014-01 • Food Back-Outs	($386.70)	-0.17%
TOTAL FOOD COST	**$74,247.13**	**32.46%**
5017 • Alcohol free beverage cost		
5017-01 • NA Bev Inventory Change	$242.15	2.53%
5017 • Alcohol free beverage cost – Other	$2,029.73	21.24%
Total 5017 • Alcohol free beverage cost	**$2,271.88**	**23.77%**
5019 • Wine cost		
5019-01 • Wine Inventory Change	($3,317.90)	-3.76%
5019 • Wine cost – Other	$24,851.50	28.17%
Total 5019 • Wine cost	**$21,533.60**	**24.41%**
5020 • Liquor cost		
5020-01 • Liquor Inventory Change	($3,928.79)	-12.16%
5020 • Liquor cost – Other	$9,363.06	28.97%
Total 5020 • Liquor cost	**$5,434.27**	**16.82%**
5021 • Beer cost		
5021-01 • Beer Inventory Change	$44.34	0.68%
5021 • Beer cost – Other	$1,703.20	26.13%
Total 5021 • Beer cost	**$1,747.54**	**26.81%**
TOTAL BEVERAGE COST	**$30,987.29**	**22.68%**
TOTAL COGS	**$105,234.42**	**28.81%**

5210 • Payroll Expense

5211 • Cooks	$18,197.05	4.98%
5212 • Bakery	$2,410.30	0.66%
5216 • Management	$32,779.23	8.97%
5217 • Dishwashers	$5,795.42	1.59%
5223 • Food runners	$1,863.25	0.51%
5225 • Hostesses/cashiers/coatroom	$3,783.68	1.04%
5226 • Waitpersons	$6,435.66	1.76%
5227 • Bus & set up	$3,124.61	0.86%
5250 • Beverage staff	$3,318.54	0.91%
5252 • Wages Wine steward	$0.00	0.00%
5260 • Sales	$470.00	0.13%
5300 • Wages Training/Meeting	$154.41	0.04%
5317 • Vacation pay	$3,022.99	0.83%
5330 • Commission – delivery	$986.80	0.27%
6150 • Administrative allocation	$9,414.00	2.58%
Salaries & Wages	**$91,755.94**	**25.13%**
6233 • FICA taxes - Employers account	$11,448.66	3.13%
6234 • SUTA tax expense	$4,040.69	1.11%
6236 • FUTA tax expense	$893.44	0.24%
6255 • Health and life insurance	$4,174.64	1.14%
6260 • Workmen's compensation	$4,670.08	1.28%
6261 • Other employee benefits	$513.00	0.14%
Employee Benefits	**$25,740.51**	**7.04%**
Total 5210 • Payroll Expense	**$117,496.45**	**32.17%**

Operating Expenses

6051 • Cleaning	$3,268.00	0.89%
6059 • Repairs & Maintenance	$1,180.00	0.32%
6060 • Other Office expense	$0.00	0.00%
6244 • China, glass, & silver	$1,053.75	0.29%
6246 • Bar supplies	$0.00	0.00%
6277 • Equipment maintenance	$955.15	0.26%
6285 • Refrigerator & air-conditioner	$685.80	0.19%
6286 • Kitchen repairs	$0.00	0.00%
6290 • Heating & air-conditioning	$1,635.00	0.45%
6329 • Advertising – coupon promotions		
6330 • Advertising – media	$1,378.67	0.38%
6332 • Advertising and promotion	$0.00	0.00%

6333 • Advertising – trade	($1,440.00)	-0.39%
6342 • Rewards Network	$3,221.59	0.88%
6345 • Promotion	$504.33	0.14%
6347 • Sales discounts	$15,170.96	4.15%
6631 • Public relations	$1,160.00	0.32%
Total 6329 • Advertising - coupon promotions	**$19,995.55**	**5.48%**
6343 • Credit card discounts	$12,184.39	3.34%
6354 • Laundry and linen	$4,177.60	1.14%

Utilities

6376 • Natural gas	$1,338.78	0.37%
6388 • Cable	$170.98	0.05%
6398 • Water	$701.02	0.19%
6399 • Sewer	$1,772.43	0.49%
6442 • Telephone	$390.28	0.11%
6365 • Electricity – Other	$3,905.60	1.07%
Total Utilities	**$8,279.09**	**2.28%**
6409 • Insurance	$2,642.19	0.72%
6420 • Cleaning supplies and expense	$1,342.86	0.37%
6421 • Restaurant and bar supplies	$2,630.81	0.72%
6422 • Kitchen smallwares	$0.00	0.00%
6423 • Catering supplies	$89.00	0.02%
6510 • Miscellaneous	$6,405.00	1.75%
6519 • Paper goods and supplies	$260.16	0.07%
6585 • Printing and stationery	$1,800.59	0.49%
6640 • Exterminating & pest control	$0.00	0.00%

7000 • Occupancy Cost

6211 • Rent	$22,500.00	6.16%
6212 • Storage	$600.00	0.16%
6216 • Common Area Maintenance	$4,341.09	1.19%
6600 • Real estate taxes	$8,030.05	2.20%
6651 • Rubbish removal	$1,229.69	0.34%
Total 7000 • Occupancy Cost	**$36,700.83**	**10.05%**
Total Operating Expense	**$105,285.77**	**28.83%**

When I'm touring individual restaurants of ours, I make sure to talk to chefs, bartenders, and others about parts of our cost structure that they influence. This keeps my people on their toes; they know I'm going to ask, so they make it their business to know about costs on a daily basis. I'm also always thinking on my own about ways to cut out waste. The other day, I was in one of our locations at 8:00 a.m. and noticed one of our salad guys setting up his station. "We don't open till 11:30," I said to myself. "What is the salad guy doing here so early?" I asked Eric, the chef, whether the salad guy really needed three hours to set up his station, and now we're looking at having him come in an hour later. That one little change will save us thousands in labor costs over the course of a year—all because I was paying attention and keeping my eyes open.

To keep all of us doing this, I also include incentives in the compensation plans I give my key people. Our head chef and sous-chef make a bonus if they keep hourly labor below 10 percent and food costs below 32 percent. Our general managers get a bonus tied to our net profit, since the decisions they make hit multiple cost areas. Now, you might ask: With all this emphasis on lowering cost, are we sacrificing quality? My job is to see that this doesn't happen. I balance out the incentives I offer by requiring that my chefs purchase supplies only from Dining Alliance companies that I *know* sell good stuff. I'm also in the restaurants all the time, looking at the food to make sure the portions aren't too small (but also not too big) and that the quality is where we need it to be. The overall point is to create a system in which all the key decision-makers act *both* like chefs who love high-quality food and like businesspeople who care about the bottom line.

You know what's cool? When you give people proper incentives, train them to look at the numbers, and hire people who understand numbers, you can create a healthy competition that makes the whole business hum. Our managers can't wait for the numbers to come out at the end of each month. "Steve," they e-mail me, "did the numbers come in yet? Are they there?" Claude, our general manager in Atlanta, never fails to say, "Steve, can I call Bob [our accountant]? I want these numbers!" This is only a few days after our accounting period closed. *Man,* I think. *Can you give Bob at least a week?* They want to see if they've improved over the previous month, or if they've beaten their colleagues at other restaurants in our company. And then the *really* fun stuff starts—they begin tearing the numbers apart looking for insights. Why does meat in our Atlanta location cost 4 percent more than in Boston? Why is hourly labor at 10 percent in Philly but only 9 percent in New York City? Why do sales dip slightly less in February in Boston than they do elsewhere? It's all interesting, it all matters, and it all can make us more money.

You might wonder why I still care about making more money at this point in my career. With so many restaurants, a $10 million packaged foods business, and other nonfood businesses, haven't I made enough? Yes . . . and no. I have a very nice lifestyle. But that just puts even more pressure on me. What I'm worried about is *keeping* what I already have. The more you have, the more you have to *lose.*

This past January, right after New Year's, I went into the restaurant and nobody was there. I practically freaked out. We had just had our busiest year ever, with large increases in sales over the previous year, and it was a day of the year when nobody eats out. All I could think was, *Oh my God. It's finally caught up to us. We're done. Nobody's coming in anymore. We're going out of business.*

I'll admit it: I'm paranoid that one day everything I've worked so hard to build will go up in smoke. I've been through tough times. I've operated through three recessions and counting. I remember what it was like in the early days when I had trouble paying guys just to come and fix our equipment. Those kinds of experiences scar you. I have friends with beautiful boats and planes, and I do let myself go away with them and enjoy myself. I also take ski weekends with my family. But I'm never gone for very long (and in any case, with modern technology I'm never really out of touch). I take *nothing* for granted. I just can't bring myself to take my eye off the money. And if you want to build something solid, something that lasts, neither will you.

Restaurant Lessons to Live By

Boobs slathered in whipped cream are great, but money is better. If you want to do well in your business, you should think the same way.

Figure out what you need to get your place up and running. Then add 25 percent. Hey, you never know.

Figure out how much it costs to make what you're selling. Otherwise, you'll be losing money without even knowing it.

Once you're up and running, watch the little things. An extra ounce of wine per glass adds up real quick.

Create a culture of money at your company. Get people involved. Keep them engaged. Watch them compete to shave even more off your cost structure.

If you're not paranoid right after New Year's, I guarantee you one of your competitors is, and he or she is going to win.

CHAPTER SEVEN

A Busy Restaurant
Is a Happy Restaurant

In talking about money, I've focused most on controlling costs. Let's look at the other side of the equation, sales. Obviously you need your eye on that, too. The real question is this: How do you get people into the restaurant—or any other business—and keep them there? How do you stay busy? How do you keep your brand strong and vibrant in your local community?

One thing you can do is get people in the media talking about you in a positive way. Back in the mid-'80s, before blogs and social media, having a food critic from a major newspaper rave about your food was critical, far more important than it is now. These guys were tastemakers. Their every word made or broke budding restaurateurs in a local market.

My first big accomplishment in this business was to get Boston's premier daily paper, the *Globe*, raving about Davio's. At first I didn't think it would happen. Being the brash young kid that I was, only twenty-four years old, I called Robert

Levey, the *Globe*'s food guy, and asked him to come eat at Davio's. This was about five months after we'd opened. "Well, I don't know," said Levey. "I'll see what I think. But I've heard about you, that you've changed everything."

"Yes, it's a whole new menu, everything's new. I only kept the name," I said, knowing that he wouldn't review a place unless something was new. And he said something, then something else, and then yes—he'd come.

I jumped right into action to prepare for his visit, making sure everything was perfect. I was obsessed! All day long, I thought to myself, "Robert Levey is coming in. Robert Levey is coming in. Maybe tonight's the night." Before dinner service I called our staff together. "Okay, we need a good review, but we don't know what Robert Levey looks like. Maybe he isn't even a guy. From now on we treat every guest like he or she is Robert Levey."

He didn't come in that night. Nor the next night. Nor the night after that. A week passed. Then another week. "This could be the night!" I kept saying. I told people to expect anything: Robert Levey might not come downstairs but just go straight to the cafe. He could be young or old, in a large group or a deuce.

On the fifteenth night Diane, a server who had just started in our upstairs cafe, came up to me. "Steve, I just started interning at the *Globe*."

"Oh, perfect," I said. "How is that going?"

She shook her head. "No, you don't understand. I know what Robert Levey looks like. I work with him pretty much every day in his office."

"What does he look like? Tell me!"

She thought about it for a moment. "Well, he's very distinguished. He has a full beard, he's got brown hair with some gray, he's probably in his late forties, and he's tall. Actually, he kind of looks like Abraham Lincoln. Yeah, that's how I would describe him."

I nodded. "Okay, here's what we're going to do. From now until when Robert Levey comes in, you have to work every night. No time off. I need you here at all times to identify Robert Levey when he comes in. Cool?"

She smiled. "Cool."

Now I had a foolproof way of identifying Robert Levey. This was great. On second thought, maybe not so great. That night, as people came in, I was a nervous nelly. I swore that each male guest looked like Abraham Lincoln. Never had I seen so many Lincoln look-alikes. Again and again, I dragged Diane downstairs to the dining room to look. "Diane! Diane! Is that him?"

Each time, she shook her head. "No, Steve, sorry." Once, she even said, "Sorry, Steve. Hey, that's a woman, okay?"

Several nights later, a guy came in with a party of four. He sat down and looked right at me. I mean, *right at me*. It was like he was telling me: "I . . . am . . . Robert . . . Levey." And he looked a bit like Abraham Lincoln, too.

"It's him!" I said to myself. I ran upstairs and tapped Diane on the shoulder. "Diane! Diane! I think this is him!"

She sighed and flashed me a doubtful look. "Really? Again?"

"I am absolutely certain this time it's him."

"Okay," she said, putting down some dishes she was carrying. "Let me go down and take a look."

She came downstairs and peeked around a corner. *"That's him!!!"* she whispered.

She and I and a couple of others ran into the kitchen, excited and jumping up and down. "Oh my God! Oh my God!"

"What are we gonna do now?" someone asked.

I pulled myself together. "Okay. What we're going to do is just make sure the food is good. I mean, absolutely perfect. We can't screw this up."

He was with three other people, and Tonino waited on them. They ordered so much, but I can't remember exactly what: several appetizers, a veal chop, I think, one of our fish dishes, a couple pastas, a few salads—and it all went well. After that he came in two more times. And a while after his third visit, he called to ask a couple questions. He told me that the review would be in the paper the day after Christmas, 1985.

The wait was excruciating. I could barely contain myself. Never had time passed so slowly. Getting a positive review from Robert Levey was the only thing in the world that mattered to me.

Just after midnight on December 26, I couldn't take it anymore, so I drove down to the *Boston Globe*'s headquarters. I pulled into the side parking lot where all the trucks back into the enormous building on Morrissey Boulevard to load the papers. Guys were hanging around. I asked one if the *Globe* had come out yet and he said it should be down in about twenty minutes.

I went back and sat in my car.

Finally, I saw people walking out with the paper and went over to my guy and asked for one. "How much do I owe you?" I asked.

He waved me off. "Obviously this means a lot to you, pal. Just take one." And he gave it to me.

I ran back to my car, ripping the paper open as I went. What I wanted to see was how many stars he gave us. Four stars was the best, but nobody ever got that. Two or two and a half stars would have been disappointing, and anything below that devastating. Three would have been a great review. And that's what we received. Three stars! I couldn't believe it. To make it even better, Levey called our restaurant "a renaissance on Newbury Street." I was on top of the world. "We did it!" I shouted out loud, tears in my eyes. "We did it!"

Levey reviewed us a bunch more times over the years as we opened new locations, and we became good friends. He saw me as his baby, an up-and-coming restaurateur that he, the food veteran, was championing. Years later, when I was well established on the Boston food scene, he invited me to go reviewing with him. That was sheer heaven for a food guy like me, right up there with having Julia Child fall asleep on me. Levey always asked me, "Hey, Steve, that first time I reviewed you, did you know it was me?" And I always told him, "Oh, no, not at all!" I could never get the courage up to tell him the truth. (I guess I just did.)

That first review changed my life. It was one of the happiest days of my life. From then on the phone rang off the hook. You couldn't get into our place. We were booked as much as a month in advance. We became permanently busy, and as the title of this chapter says, a busy restaurant is a happy restaurant.

You may have guessed that I was a marketing lunatic. I majored in marketing at Boston University and am still crazy about the subject. These days, I have a bunch of other marketing lunatics working with me. Why? Lots of restaurants have terrific food and great service, but they still don't make it. Davio's has remained one of the top-grossing restaurants in each of its markets, per square foot, because of our teams' ceaseless, hit-the-streets, grassroots marketing efforts.

Think of it this way: The minute a restaurant loses guests, morale drops among the staff, and everything else—product quality, service, guest satisfaction—goes downhill fast. A similar dynamic holds true for any business. So you can't ever lose momentum. If you're starting your own business, you have to push hard with marketing at the beginning and keep pushing hard. Never let success make you complacent. Keep trying new things to get butts in your chairs. When those new things get old, try even more new things. It's the only way.

Getting a business off the ground is tricky. If you can afford it, I would advise working with a public relations firm. When I open a new Davio's, I'm swamped with the operational details, yet I also need to get in front of the right media personalities—food critics, bloggers, and the like—with credibility in the local area. All kinds of local media outlets and promotional companies call me up, looking to work with us. I have to find where to spend our money to be most effective.

A good PR firm is in my corner to give me strategic and tactical advice. Regan Communications in Boston is the firm I use, and I think they're top-notch. "No," my account executive Joanna says, "you don't want to bother with that. Do this instead." PR firms also help tremendously by getting people into the restaurant, and not just anybody—people who matter.

When you're opening a new venue, you get one shot. If the public hears the restaurant isn't busy, you've got a stigma. So you've got to come out guns blazing. You've got to get *noticed.* And that means you have to think of every last tactic, every event, everything to get trendsetters and celebrities to try you out. PR firms know what to do and who to call. Why do the Yankees come to my new restaurant? Because my PR firm knows the right people. Why's the governor eating there? Same reason.

It goes beyond that. One of our biggest launch tactics is to cultivate those in a position to bring large events into our restaurants. Who's the big law firm executive around here, who's the guy who entertains, who are the meeting planners who do all the functions? PR firms in a local area are plugged into the scene and can help us make business connections much faster than we could on our own.

Shortly after I opened my Philadelphia Davio's in 1999, I brought a small PR firm on board, and it did killer work. The newspapers wrote about us. We were on TV and radio all the time. We did all sorts of cooking events. It was great—and it made all the difference in our success. After a while we took over PR duties ourselves, because we thought we could handle it. In 2010, realizing we needed help again, I hired a local PR firm called Image Unlimited, and we got another boost—a 15 percent rise in sales within three to six months. It was huge! I was so impressed and happy that I wound up stealing away Anny, our rep at Image Unlimited, and making her the PR and marketing director for our whole company. Because of my sales at that point, I could afford to do something like that; years earlier, I would have stuck with a local PR firm, something that I would advise any start-up restaurant to do.

When I first started out, I didn't even know what a PR firm was. If you're operating on a shoestring, you can still do a lot of the same stuff yourself, so long as you or other people on the team are plugged into your local market. If you want to know the events people who book big parties in a city, you can go to the *Boston Business Journal* or similar journals in other major cities and you'll find long lists of people to call. It will take you forever to go down the list, and you might not have much luck without personal introductions, but you can certainly make a go of it without a PR company.

As far as social media goes, the sky's the limit. If you've got more technical know-how than I do, you can have a blast sending e-mail newsletters out and running contests. Our newsletter routinely announces upcoming special events, cooking classes, and special promotions. It's incredible how much response we get. We run a contest every year asking people to come up with a recipe for a new spring roll. The lucky winner, selected by our chefs, gets his or her name on the menu for two weeks as well as a free family dinner. One contestant came up with a macaroni and cheese spring roll that was so good, we developed its recipe and now sell that flavor in supermarkets.

Lately, I've been spending more and more time tweeting, and I love it. (By the way, you can follow me @stevedifillippo.)

I also like to keep up with all the latest blogs and dot-coms. I'm not a Facebook guy, simply because I don't have time for everything. Instead, I have members of my team maintain Facebook pages for our individual restaurants. It has a direct impact on our sales. In 2013 we got thirty inches of snow in one night, which closed the lifestyle center where our Foxboro restaurant is located. We were the only business, besides the movie theater, that decided to stay open. We knew that we could tweet and post on Facebook that we were open, and some would brave the poor roads and come. We were right—that night proved to be extremely busy.

Heading off-line, you can't go wrong cultivating concierges at local hotels. When I was a kid traveling with my dad on business, we would eat only at Italian restaurants. If we were in a city for a few days, we'd try four different Italian joints. But we chose those places by going to the concierge and asking for recommendations. I marveled at how much influence the concierges had over my dad. Anyone could recommend a restaurant, but if the concierge at the Ritz said it was good— well, we had to go. "Who are these guys that have such power?" I asked myself.

When I started Davio's I told myself that I needed to get to these concierge gods. I couldn't just bring them food; I needed them to come to Davio's and experience it for themselves, so they would recommend it wholeheartedly. I also knew I needed to make this outreach continuous, since in some hotels concierge staffs have a lot of turnover. And that's what I did. I went everywhere: the Ritz, the Four Seasons, the Marriott, the Sheraton, the Westin, the Park Plaza, the Copley Plaza, and others even farther afield. I went in, introduced myself, told them about the new Davio's, and invited them to come eat a meal on us. I didn't go just once; I went often, week after week, getting to know each of them, until I'd finally get them in. And they sent us business, a lot of business, and still do.

I'm not sure if my competitors put the lock on concierges. I have to think that they do. It's such a powerful, effective way to get people in. Today, we ply concierges with gift cards, bake them cookies, and invite them in for dinner. Almost instantly—like, *that night*—we'll see three or four tables coming our way from that hotel. Here's a dish the concierges love. If you like lobster, you *have* to try the one on page 118.

One day, I was getting my hair cut on Newbury Street, and I noticed that everyone around me was talking—women, men, everyone. Hairdressers as a group (my stylist Janet excepted) never shut up; all they do is talk, talk, talk (and drink, drink, drink, but that's another story). It's kind of annoying, actually, but also funny. Newbury Street has tons of salons, so I thought, *Why don't we get them all to try our food so they'll talk about us?* We brought them pizza and coupons, and sure enough, it was a huge marketing success. We got a noticeable uptick in business. Many of them even started to hang out and drink at our bar.

Another great tactic, with or without the help of a PR firm, is cultivating local radio and television personalities. When we first opened, our cook Ralph Bryant bumped into a guy from WBCN—which was one of the country's most popular

Pan-Roasted Maine Lobster
with Lemon-Tarragon Butter Sauce

For this recipe you need **4 (1¼–1½ pound) whole live Maine lobsters.** Take 1 lobster and place it on a cutting board. Using an 8- to 10-inch chef's knife, place the tip of the knife behind the eyes of the lobster. I know this sounds pretty brutal, but push the knife down all the way through the lobster. Next, with the tip of the knife, remove the claws where they attach at the body. (Relax! You're almost done!) Cut the tail from the body and then cut the body in half lengthwise and remove the head sac. Repeat with the 3 remaining lobsters.

Next, we need to cook the lobster in two separate batches. For the first batch heat **2 tablespoons extra virgin olive oil** (Monini preferred) in a 12-inch skillet over high heat. Add half the lobster pieces, cut side down, and cook for 1 minute. Flip over, sprinkle with **sea salt and pepper,** and cook the shell side for another minute. Reserve the pieces on a platter. Repeat the process, starting with the olive oil and leaving the final batch of lobster in the skillet after cooking the shell side. Return the reserved lobster pieces to the skillet. Add **1 cup brandy** and let it evaporate. Then add **½ cup lobster or fish stock,** cover the skillet, lower the heat to medium, and allow all the lobster pieces to cook for an additional 5 minutes. Transfer the lobster pieces to a platter and set aside. Add **5 tablespoons unsalted butter** to the reserved skillet and heat over medium-high. Add **4 shallots, chopped,** and cook about 3 minutes until they're nice and soft. Add **½ cup heavy cream** and scrape in the reserved juices with a rubber spatula. Raising the heat to high, bring to a boil. Reduce the juices until slightly thickened. Add the lobster meat along with **2 tablespoons chopped fresh parsley, 2 tablespoons chopped fresh tarragon,** and **2 tablespoons chopped fresh chives.** Heat through. Add a nice **squeeze of lemon** and **salt and pepper** if desired. Serve with creamy mashed potatoes and haricot verts.

rock radio stations—at a party and mentioned Davio's. And the guy—I think it was the DJ, Charles Laquidara—suggested that we bring some food into the station. The next day, when Ralph told me about the conversation, I called 'BCN right away and went over with a bunch of food. And the next thing you know, all the DJs were talking about how great Davio's is. Thousands of people listening to the station heard about the restaurant and started coming in, including a lot of musicians.

Among them were Peter Wolf, Seth Justman, and Magic Dick of the J. Geils Band, who all lived within minutes of Davio's. The Cars were around then, too—the drummer, Dave Robinson, lived on our block. We were basically his coffee shop; he was there every day. He would come in and hang out with other musicians. And when these guys' friends were on tour in town, they'd bring them in. It didn't take a rocket scientist to see the power of it, because everywhere I went people would say, "Hey, I heard about you guys on 'BCN."

Meanwhile, there was a recording studio on Newbury Street that CBS Records (which later became Sony Music Entertainment) used often. After producing a new album, they'd hold listening events at the studio and book our whole upstairs cafe for parties. John Madison, CBS Records' local executive in the Boston area, loved Davio's and helped put us on the map with other big stars. We had Stevie Ray Vaughan, Joan Jett, Journey, and so many others eat our food. It all created a big buzz for Davio's because people would hear about what was going on and it made them want to come into the restaurant.

I can't tell you how many hundreds of times since then we've brought in food to radio and television studios, both on our own and working with PR firms. Over the years, I've found that this tactic has led me to become friends with a number of media people, which in itself is a good thing. Initially we bring them food, then they come in the restaurant, and over time I hang out with them. One Boston sportscaster, Glenn Ordway, has become such a good friend that I'm godfather to his son Sam!

Beyond the genuine personal satisfaction I get from these relationships, I find that they lead to other really cool business and media opportunities. I had been a guest on *TV Diner*—a Boston-area food show on the NECN cable network hosted by my good friend Billy Costa—many times when I was approached by the owner of a different show, *Style Boston*. Would I be interested in hosting my own food segment on that show? I asked Billy if he minded, and he thought it was a great chance to get Davio's more exposure. "Go ahead, do it!" he said. That's Billy—a guy who really cares about people and looks out for them. As of this writing, the twenty-five segments I've done have given me a much higher profile in the Boston area. People at home—as many as 50,000 of them for a given show—see me on television and say to themselves, "Wow, I want to be a part of that. I want to go to that restaurant. I want to know that guy." And lo and behold, they come in.

✐

Getting in the media is only part of the restaurateur's larger work of talking to people in the local community and being seen. I try to go to as many social events or benefits as I can and meet as many people as possible. I'm so visible week in and week out—because I make it my business to be—that people come up to me all the time and say, "Gee, Steve, if I don't see you in the paper, I think you're sick!" Everywhere I go, I bring business cards with me, since I always seem to run into people who know me or Davio's. You should never leave your house without cards! I'll go to Costco with cards and people ask me for them. Every minute is a potential marketing opportunity. You have to *constantly* sell yourself.

Once I was on an airplane, and wanting to play some music, I opened the case in which I keep my Bose headset. I happened to have a couple of spare cards in there. A nosy passenger sitting next to me said, "Oh, Davio's, I love that restaurant. Do you work there?" He wound up taking my card and coming in that night! From then on I made sure to always have a couple of cards in that headset case.

Another time, my wife and I were at the Four Seasons, riding the elevator up to a charity event we were attending. A guy nearby said to me, "Hey, we're going out to eat this weekend. Is there any place you recommend?"

"Yeah, you gotta go to Davio's!"

"Oh, great, great," the guy said.

"Yeah, go ask the concierges and see what they say. I bet they'll say, 'Go to Davio's.'"

We got off the elevator and my wife shook her head at me. "I can't believe you just did that."

I laughed. "That's what I do."

Good thing, too. A couple of nights later, I was working in the restaurant when the guy showed up. "Hey!" he said.

"You're the guy from the elevator! Now I know why you said Davio's; you work here!"

It turned out that he *had* asked the concierge, and she had enthusiastically recommended us. It just goes to show you that a thirty-second conversation coupled with all we do cultivating concierges really does work magic.

You also can't go wrong by simply being in the restaurants and forging relationships with the guests. I've had so many memorable interactions with guests over the years—including hundreds, maybe thousands of celebrities who have come in, people like Bruce Springsteen, Oprah Winfrey, Vice President Joe Biden, Ringo Starr, Mick Jagger, Derek Jeter, Kevin Youkilis, Joe Torre, and Mark Wahlberg. But my most memorable encounters haven't been with celebrities. One night at our original Newbury Street location, I was standing near the entrance when I noticed one of our regulars open the outer door and then shove it closed and walk back up the stairs that led to the street. He did this three times. What was going on? I finally went out there and said to the man, "Oh, Mr. Farrell, it's you." I looked up the stairs. "Where's your wife?"

His eyes were puffy and he looked terribly sad. "She's dead, Steve. She's dead!"

"Oh, I'm so sorry. I had no idea. I wish I had known." I was really embarrassed. It was a rookie mistake, like asking an overweight woman if she was pregnant.

We both started crying. I put my arm around him. "Come in and have dinner. Tonino, Alan, and Howard would love to see you. I'll sit with you." I did that. We had dinner together and he just kept crying. It turned out that he had wanted to come back in so badly to our restaurant, but he just couldn't. He needed me to stay with him and help him feel like it was okay to be spending time at Davio's without his wife—that he still had a place with us. It was then that I saw how powerful restaurants could be to people. I could have said, "To hell with this guy. Who cares if his wife died?" But that's not how we are, and it's also why Davio's continues to have such an incredible base of loyal guests. For Mr. Farrell, that night was a turning point. He has since overcome his grief and even started dating.

Developing relationships with guests can also come back to haunt you if you're not careful—and even if you are careful. Let me tell you one of the greatest stories in the *history* of stories. In 1997 a doctor who treated my first wife—let's call him Dr. Tannenbaum—was building a house in the Boston suburb of Brookline. Like everyone else, he asked me if I knew a good contractor, and I highly recommended a guy who had built my own house and a couple of my restaurants. "Hire him," I said. "Don't even give it a second thought. He's fantastic! And his nephew Larry, who works as the foreman, is also unbelievably good." Dr. Tannenbaum, a brilliant guy and extremely talented, hired them based on my enthusiasm.

I went about my life and forgot the encounter. Months went by. A year. One night, I was working the door at our location in Brookline when the phone rang. "Good evening, Davio's," I said.

"Is Steve there?" asked the guy on the other end.

"Yes, this is Steve."

"Hi, Steve. This is Dr. Tannenbaum."

"Oh, hey, Doc. How are you doing tonight? I haven't seen you in so long!"

Awkward silence. "Oh. Yeah. You know why you haven't seen me."

"No," I said, "I have no idea."

"You know why."

"I swear, I don't!"

"C'mon. You don't?"

"Really, doctor, I have no idea why you haven't been in."

Another pause. "'Cause Larry is fucking my wife!"

I nearly dropped the phone. I couldn't believe this. Larry the foreman? Who was married to a beautiful woman and had four kids? And I had recommended the guy! It was all my fault!

I didn't know what to do. For one of the few times I can think of, I was utterly stunned speechless.

"You've ruined my life, Steve. You've ruined it, okay?"

"I'm so sorry, doctor. Really. I don't know what else to say."

"You can go fuck yourself!" And he hung up on me.

I was shaken up for a long time. I had always tried to build relationships with my guests, and here, with my recommendation, I had ruined an entire family. Two families.

But the story doesn't end there. Four years later, I was in a Star Market in Gloucester, Massachusetts, looking at the avocados, and there they were—Larry and the doctor's wife. Larry came up to me, and after an awkward moment we began chatting. It turned out that this woman, who indeed was quite beautiful, wasn't the doctor's wife any longer. She and the doctor had gotten a divorce, and Larry had left his wife. All because little old me had been trying to stay rooted in the community. I had tried to become acquainted with my guests and help them as much as I could.

Today, with restaurants in multiple states, I can't hope to remain a presence in each one. That's where my general managers come in. In Boston I have Efrain; in Atlanta I have

Claude; in Philly I have Ettore; in Lynnfield I have Joe; in Foxborough I have Paul; in Chestnut Hill I have Oliver; in New York City I have Doss. All of them stay extremely visible and rooted in the local communities, forging relationships with our guests. We also try to hire as many managers, servers, and other staff with ties to the community as possible. Restaurants should all be neighborhood businesses. If you have staff from the local area serving guests, they'll all be able to recognize that local weatherman or news anchor who comes in.

One night, Robert Kraft, owner of the New England Patriots, dropped in for dinner. Our young host came up to me and said, "I just sat this guy by the bar, and he looks really familiar. I think he might know you."

I went out to look at him and practically had a heart attack. "What?! Are you kidding me? You sat Robert Kraft in the bar?"

"Well, Steve, I didn't know he was important."

"Couldn't you have just held on a second and come and gotten me?"

We had nearly missed a chance to please Mr. Kraft and give him personalized treatment. What a tragedy that would have been! That's when I understood: At the very least, you need to have someone stationed at the door, preferably a general manager, who is from the local area and knows what's what. And preferably, you'll have a whole team of people like that. We do, which is one reason we've been able to please the many local as well as national and international celebrities who visit us, so that they, too, want to come back—and bring their friends.

Although getting embedded in a local community benefits the bottom line, it isn't and shouldn't be a one-way street. Restaurants need to act as responsible players in the communities they serve. It's just the right thing for them to do—besides it being great for business.

I think of myself as one of the most fortunate people in the world. I was lucky to grow up in an incredible family that didn't have to worry about where its next meals were coming from, and whose members were generally happy and healthy. Now that I've been successful, it's my duty to make sure that I use the money I make to raise up others who are suffering. At the same time, I'm running a business. We spend many tens of thousands of dollars each year on charitable causes and participate in many, many charity events every month—and it has contributed greatly to our success. The principle is simple, and it applies to any business: You have to give to get. Give more, you get more.

If you're a guest looking to dine out and you know that we supported your kid's fund-raiser last year, where are you going to go first to make reservations? You're going to say, "Hey, why don't I call Claude at Davio's? He sure did a good thing by supporting our fund-raiser." Add to that the hundreds of potential guests I'll meet over the course of an evening out at a benefit dinner. It's a great way to get into people's minds, complementing the broader, less personal media and public relations outreach we do.

I didn't initially pursue charity work as a marketing strategy; I kind of fell into it. As a kid I had seen my mom becoming involved with the Home for Little Wanderers, an organization that helps underprivileged children and their families. When

I opened Davio's people from local organizations started calling in and asking me for donations of gift cards, so I gave it a try. I began to investigate where the money was going and saw that I really could help people and do good. My donations helped kids do things like learn how to cook and get a job. We hired inner-city interns and saw what a difference that made in their lives. It hit me that restaurants have a role to play— that we *can* be important and change the world. It's incredible what restaurants can do for local communities just by being there: bring down crime, build up other local businesses, give people jobs, contribute to the social fabric.

Today, we help charitable causes in many ways, including holding food events, donating gift cards, and sponsoring charity benefits. I prefer to become involved with smaller organizations, since the big ones already have plenty of help. Also, I like to see where my money is going and know firsthand that I've made a difference. For example, Davio's helped raise millions of dollars for a foundation named for Anthony Spinazzola (the *Boston Globe*'s food critic prior to Robert Levey) and run by Anthony's son Chris. Now disbanded, the foundation did a lot of good with food-related causes, taking kids from the inner city and bringing them into restaurants like ours for internships. The foundation also helped local Boston shelters like Rosie's Place and the Pine Street Inn.

Other charities I'm involved with also hold personal meaning. My sister is the executive director of a group called Raising a Reader MA that takes books to underprivileged, inner-city kids, people whose families have trouble putting food on the table. The last thing these families are thinking about is buying books, but reading is essential to a kid's growth. Every

Friday, Donna's organization takes three or four books in a red bag and leaves them with the families. They also hold seminars to teach parents how to read to their kids. And then there's BUILD, a group that takes at-risk kids from Boston high schools and coaches them to start their own businesses. A group of these teenagers gets together every week to plan and run a company, under the guidance of a mentor. So far, 100 percent of participants in this program have gone on to college. Given my own experiences in business, I enjoy being part of BUILD—giving back and feeling like I have a lot to share. I love seeing the difference I'm making.

Sometimes charity can lead to some really great, nationwide exposure. For a couple of years now, I have been privileged to do an event called Taste of the NFL the night before the Super Bowl. One chef from each NFL city is chosen to go to the Super Bowl and represent the city at a tasting before three thousand people; I have represented Boston and the New England Patriots. Prior to the event itself, each chef raises money that Taste of the NFL matches and that ultimately goes back to food banks in the chef's home city. The first year I did it, the Patriots were competing in the Super Bowl against the New York Giants, so the New York chef and myself went head-to-head in a slider competition. That landed me some great publicity—two interviews on the *Today* show with Al Roker and Ann Curry. How perfect was this? A national event, national exposure, but also an ability to touch local lives— we raised $25,000 each year for the Boston food bank—and become associated with a popular local sports team. As far as marketing and brand building goes, it doesn't get much better than that.

As a side note, Taste of the NFL gave me a chance to experience my very own fifteen minutes of fame. While I was on stage at the *Today* show, people around me were clamoring for my autograph. Later, at the Taste of the NFL event itself, people threw aprons in my face, asking me to sign them using a magic marker. I complied, adding "Davio's Boston" under my name, but it all struck me as pretty weird. I said to one of the fans, "You don't have the slightest idea who I am, do you?" The guy shook his head. "No, I don't, but you're on the *Today* show, so you must be famous." Actually, I wasn't, but thanks to the show, I might have gotten just a little bit *more* famous, and Davio's probably got a few more guests in each of its markets. One thing is certain: Sales of our frozen food products at BJs skyrocketed after I mentioned them on the show.

There are many ways to give back—and also help your restaurant's local brand—besides charity. I do my best to support fellow restaurateurs. Why? First of all, because I just love restaurants—period. The more restaurants that are out there, the more fun and interesting life is! But also because all restaurants, no matter how upscale, fancy, or famous, are neighborhood establishments. We do well when other restaurants nearby do well. It is far better to be a part of a whole, thriving district of restaurants and nightlife than to be off on your own isolated little island. I've known this ever since I was a kid, going to eat out in Providence's Federal Hill district, which was teeming with Italian restaurants. Competition isn't a zero-sum game, like many people think. When one restaurant fails it's bad for everyone, because it's contagious. I believe in friendly competition, in helping each other, so that everybody wins.

When I opened Davio's I joined neighborhood groups like the Back Bay Association and the Newbury Street League, as well as bigger, statewide groups like the Massachusetts Restaurant Association. Over the years, I've also helped individual restaurateurs get started or make it through tight spots. The way I see it, it's far better to have unique, local establishments that really mean something and care about the community than national chains, which often are disconnected from the community and don't care. If I can help the little guys, I will—especially since I'm now in a better position financially to do it.

Marc Orfaly, who twenty years ago worked as one of our line cooks, today owns the Boston restaurant Pigalle. He constantly calls me for advice about his lease, new locations he wants to open, marketing ideas—anything and everything. Sometimes I think I talk to the guy more than to my own kids! I'm not complaining—I love talking to Marc. In fact, he was one of the people who inspired me to write this book, on account of all the questions he has asked me over the years.

Most recently, Marc ran into a little trouble over the Thanksgiving holiday when one of his guests posted a negative review on Facebook. She claimed, going into some detail, that his pumpkin pie tasted like vomit. Unfortunately, Marc responded by telling her in a posted message to go fuck herself. As a result, the episode got picked up in the media, giving the woman an even wider audience. Too bad Marc didn't talk to me until the day *after* he sent his message. When we did speak my advice to him was to apologize, simmer down, and let the whole thing blow over. He didn't want to—he was so upset that the guest had complained on Facebook without even presenting her issue to him in the restaurant. I could see his point; he works twenty-hour days, does a great job, and the one time he happens to make a little mistake, the guest can't even respect him enough to give him a chance to fix the problem. In the end Marc did let the episode go, passing up a chance to appear on *Today*. Within a few days, and after maybe twenty or thirty frantic calls to me, the storm blew over and everything was back to normal.

Not that long ago, two young guys who had just bought a top Boston-area restaurant from my friend Felix came to me for help. These guys saw how successful my spring roll business was, so they said, "Hey, like twenty years ago, Felix used to make this chocolate cake that people loved. We were wondering if you could help us bring it back and market it as a product." I didn't really know these people; I could have told them to go take a hike. What was in it for me? Instead I said, "Okay, sure, I'll come see you next week." I did, and they reminded me of how I was in my mid-twenties, so eager and energetic and passionate. I told them to come visit me in our factory and we'd talk about how they could get started and maybe introduce that cake to some stores.

One of the great things about helping other restaurateurs is that these little favors always come back to you. I have a term for helping people out: I call it *pocket favors*, because I always have favors from them that I can count on in my pocket, when I need them. I know that if I'm doing a tasting event for a charity and need ten or fifteen restaurants in Boston or Philly or Atlanta to participate, I can always get enough people. All I need to do is call and ask, because I have pocket favors from these guys, thanks to things I've done over the years for them.

Marketing lies at the core of what a restaurateur does. Over the years, as I've gotten deeper into it, I've found that I love engaging with people, building relationships, being known and respected in the community. It's a really fun part of my job! If you want to succeed in this business, you have to find a marketing style and promotional tactics of your own. You need to get out there and spread the word about your brand so that more and more people come in and check you out. If you like food but don't like marketing so much, then maybe you're going into the wrong business. At the very least, I'd advise you to find a partner who *does* like promoting your brand and, better yet, is great at it.

With all the different marketing activities I do, I still care *a lot* about getting good reviews from the food critics. In fact, I have my own little good-luck ritual. Just like the time I was waiting for my first review, I go out in the middle of the night to get the paper as soon as it comes out of the loading garage. It hasn't failed me yet.

Once, while I was sitting in the parking lot in a bad section of town waiting for a review in the *Boston Herald,* a prostitute knocked on my window. She wore tight leggings, a short skirt, and high heels. "Honey, you looking for a date?" I assured her I wasn't. Actually, what I said was, "No way, get away from me!" I started my car and drove a few hundred yards down the street to park there. The only thing I was after, and still am after, is someone important in the media saying we're great and worth visiting. I want to keep my restaurants alive, making money, and humming with people. I want them busier—and happier—than ever.

Restaurant Lessons to Live By

Robert Levey. Robert Levey. Robert Levey! If you want the critics to love you, make it your obsession to please them.

Don't screw up your initial opening. You get one chance. Market the hell out of yourself!

Concierge gods and hairdressers—you gotta love them.

Build personal relationships with your guests. Just try not to screw up their marriages.

You have to give to get. And what's more fulfilling than helping out the community?

CHAPTER EIGHT

Why It's Not All About the Chef

I was recently at a very special dinner hosted by one of the country's most celebrated chefs, who is a good friend of mine. It was a $1,000-a-plate, fifteen-course extravaganza held at my friend's well-known restaurant on the occasion of its fifteenth anniversary. Each magnificent course came paired with bottle after bottle of outstanding wine. Yet the event was far from a success. By only 10:00 p.m. half the people had left although the meal was not even two-thirds over.

Why? Because a chef was running the evening and was too busy cooking to focus on managing or hosting it.

I love my friend to death, and he's a super-talented guy, but he should have known that you can't have an event mid-week that goes beyond 10:00 p.m. People need to go home and get to bed so that they can get up for work the next day. The courses should have moved along faster or come out two at a time. Someone should have sensed what the group needed and made adjustments. My friend didn't do any of this. He spent most of his time in the kitchen and didn't work the room. Big mistake.

Can I rant for a moment about some chefs and their attitudes? I like to say that they have a street named after chefs. It's called "One Way." All chefs think about is the food. If the food is excellent, they think their job is done. Now keep in mind, *I* love food. I think about food every minute! I'm a food guy and always have been. But a successful restaurant is not just about food. Ever eat a meal out and discover that the food is amazing but the rest of the experience stinks? Lots of guests will bypass a place with excellent food, choosing instead a place where they can relax, enjoy, have fun, and receive great service. To succeed restaurateurs must think about guests and inner guests as well as food. They must know the whole operation. A similar statement applies to the owners of any business. A successful landscaping business, for instance, isn't just about cutting the grass, but about providing strong customer service, maintaining the company's equipment properly, getting the right people on staff, and many other things.

Many chefs look down on management tasks that take them outside the kitchen. Wow, do they have it wrong. You might be able to cook well, even handle the money, but making it in this business requires that you wear every hat from time to time: coach, maintenance guy, server, busser, host, receptionist, chef, grill, sauté, salad guy, dishwasher, HVAC expert, taster and approver, manager, salesman, ideas man, PR and HR person, garbage picker-upper, and the list goes on.

As your company grows you need to step into these roles even more often in order to stay in touch with the brand and connect with your people. And that means getting out of the office. At Davio's, we have a corporate office, and I might go there two times a year. I don't have a desk of my own, just a leather bag with papers in it that I carry around. When I meet with people, it's at a table in one of our locations. Offices don't make money, and I didn't get into this business to work in one. I want to be where our guests and inner guests are.

In any large business, whether it's manufacturing, sales, or healthcare, leaders can't succeed if they hole themselves up in their executive suites, thinking they're above everyone else. There's no room for big egos, so if you're starting or growing a business, I advise that you lose the attitude, get in the trenches, and get your hands dirty. Only then will you have a well-managed business that pleases guests, keeps team members on their toes, and most important, *stays open.*

<hr />

One of the biggest reasons to get outside the kitchen or executive suite is to identify threats to the brand experience. Just after we opened the Newbury Street restaurant, I was working the door one night and a guest lit up this huge stogie. This was in 1989, when you could smoke in restaurants. Still, a stogie? This was a small restaurant, and a car driving by could smell this cigar, it was so awful. After the guy had paid his bill, I went up to him and said, "Sir, you can't smoke a cigar in here. You're going to bother everybody. Would you mind taking it outside?"

The man looked at me like I was nuts. "I just spent $200. If I want to smoke a fucking cigar, I'm gonna smoke."

Oh. My. God.

"Sir," I said, "if you spent $1,000, does that mean you get to take the chair with you? Everyone in this room is spending money."

He stood up. "Really? Well, we're gonna leave."

"Well, maybe that's the best thing." He and his friend were finished with their meals anyway. And I couldn't have them bothering other guests.

But this man didn't just leave. He made a big show of it, blowing smoke around the room as he walked to the door, stopping to make a whole smoke cloud before stepping outside. When he was gone everyone clapped. I still remember what that sounded like, some twenty-five years later. It was so great.

We didn't have general managers then—we were too small. If I hadn't been there keeping an eye on things, who's to say a server would have asked the man to leave, or stood up to him when he refused? It was up to me that night to protect our dining experience and our brand. I didn't want us to be known as that place on Newbury Street that tolerated cigar smoke. I wanted us to be known as a place where you could come and enjoy a fun, high-quality dining experience. While breathing clean air.

The applause of the crowd that night made such an impression on me that after this incident, I banned all smoking in our downstairs dining room—a full fifteen years before Massachusetts law required it. I had been an avid nonsmoker and had gotten some of my team members to give up the habit. I was afraid that banning smoking would hurt business, but in fact it helped business. A lot of people wanted to eat dinner without taxing their lungs and smelling up their clothes, and few if any restaurants in Boston at the time allowed for this. We still allowed smoking upstairs at the bar, so if someone really wanted to smoke, they had that option.

It's so important in business to be constantly on the prowl, talking to guests and team members, cultivating an active and engaged management style. There is simply no substitute for paying attention to operations and how you can improve them. It's about understanding guests, but more broadly, protecting the brand.

By the way, here's what that obnoxious cigar guy probably should have ordered for dessert, if he hadn't been in such a hurry to leave.

Panna Cotta

Before you do anything else, prep 15 (4-ounce) aluminum tins or molds. Pour enough **amber caramel** to just cover the bottom of each tin, and then set them aside. Take **3⅓ cups heavy cream, ¾ cup sugar, 2 strips orange zest,** and **1 scraped vanilla bean** and bring to a boil in a 3-quart saucepan over medium heat. Remove from heat, and then stir in **1½ teaspoons powdered gelatin** and allow it to melt. Throw in **1 cup milk.** Let this mixture steep until cool and then pour it through a fine strainer. Divide the liquid among the prepared tins. Refrigerate overnight. (I know, wait an entire day!?) The next day, invert onto a plate. A little trick: Pierce the bottom of the mold to release. And there you go, panna cotta!

Often it's not guest behavior that threatens your brand, but your own people. In 2003 we hired this Italian guy from Boston's North End to wait tables for us at our new and much larger location on Arlington Street. As I mentioned in chapter three, we'll make anything for a guest, even if it's not on the menu. Veal parm is most definitely *not* on the menu, for the same reason chicken parm isn't. They're American-Italian inventions that you can find anywhere, and in some places they use low-quality cuts of meat. We're Northern Italian, and we use high-quality cuts. The veal we use for our dishes is veal tenderloin, the best veal you could possibly imagine. It would be a crime—*a crime!*—to smother our veal in cheese and sauce. But we'll make it for you if you want it, because that's what we do.

Anyhow, I'm in the restaurant one night working as an expeditor (bringing hot dishes to tables), and I notice that Giuseppe, our new server from the North End, keeps submitting orders for veal parm. It had been the same thing all week on tables this guy served—veal parm, veal parm, veal parm. He probably had taken fifteen orders for veal parm that week, more than we'd had in years. I'm surprised our chefs Eric and Steve didn't kill the guy! I went up to Giuseppe and said, "Hey, can I ask you a question? Why do you keep getting veal parms? I don't understand it. Hardly anyone ever asks for it, but for some reason you always get veal parms."

He shrugged his shoulders. "Well, I recommend it."

I couldn't believe what I was hearing. "What do you mean you recommend it? Why would you do that?"

"Well, the menu here sucks, so I think you should have veal parm on the menu."

"I'm sorry, *what?*" I was blown away. We were standing in the middle of a restaurant with 250 seats; the place was a zoo, and you couldn't even get a table. Did this guy just say our menu sucks?

"Yeah, you should have veal parm on the menu. This is an Italian restaurant."

"Well, not really, it's an Italian, we're not American . . ." And as I was getting these words out, I was thinking, *Why the hell am I defending myself?* So I stopped. Waving my hands, I said, "You know what? Forget it. Come with me." I walked Giuseppe over to our time clock and signed him out. "You're leaving right now. Give me the receipts and credit card slips from your tables."

I fired him on the spot—the first time I had ever done that, and hopefully the last time, too. I was just so mad. He thought we were a typical American-Italian restaurant. I love American-Italian places and eat at them often. But Davio's had always been different, because I had wanted us to stand out with dishes you can't enjoy elsewhere. We had worked so hard over so many years by that point to become known first as a Northern Italian restaurant, and by 2002 as a Northern Italian steakhouse. Giuseppe was telling our guests to order something that ran totally counter to our brand. Not to mention that he was downright rude to me. How would he behave with a guest he didn't like?

One thing's for certain: If I had been locked in the kitchen all night cooking or in an office somewhere, or if I had thought that being the expeditor that evening was beneath me, I never would have noticed this clown and his veal parm shenanigans. He would still be working for us, and who knows, today we might be known as the veal parm restaurant. What a thought!

Taking the time to notice things is such a vital life skill. My father used to preach it to me, and now I do the same to my own kids. I tell them all the time: Wherever you go, you should be looking around, paying attention. My son Max has gotten the message. A couple of years ago, I was with him and my other three kids in a shoe store in Boston called the Tannery, owned by a man named Sam who likes to come eat at Davio's. Sam sells the best clogs, and because I talk up his store a lot, he takes care of me, never letting me pay. On this day he gave us three pairs of clogs and told me to put away my credit card. He gave me a warm hug and kissed me three or four times, and I tried to pay again. "Don't, you're embarrassing me," he said. As we left the store and were walking down the street, Max said, "Dad, all you had to do was kiss him and he gave you all those clogs for free?"

How cool, I thought. None of my older kids (Katherine, Michael, and Ella, who ranged from fifteen to twenty-five at the time) had noticed that Sam hadn't let me pay. "You know, Max," I told him, "it's really great that you observed that." I was like Max when I was his age. Nothing got by me. I watched everything. And as a restaurateur, I still do.

When I think of how I spend my time each day, I actually have a new title for myself: Noticer-in-Chief. That's my job. On a typical day I arrive at 9:00 or 10:00 a.m. at one of our restaurants and do a walk-through, inspecting the physical plant—the floor, the ceilings, the doors, the tables, the chairs. I look at the ice machine first (since the last thing we want to do is run out of ice). I talk to the bartender, the kitchen crew, and by about 10:30, the servers. I sit in the dining room at different tables, look at the chairs and walls, and try to see what the guests see. I'm taking notes, saying to myself, "Okay, we need to paint better. The rug has a funny smell—when's the last time we cleaned it?" Sometime during the morning, I go up to the general manager or manager on duty and we talk about things to work on. If for some reason I don't arrive until the afternoon on a given day, I might even grab the general manager to do the inspection with me.

By around 11:00 a.m., when the staff eats lunch, my phone is starting to go off, so I'll be fielding calls and e-mails from our PR people, our accountant, my attorney, the designer of our restaurants, or general managers from other restaurants. All along, I'm paying attention to the details of what people are saying, their tone of voice, and I'm thinking about how it affects the guest experience. When our lunch service opens, I'm out on the floor, standing at the door to greet guests. If I want to see what's going on with the food, I serve as expediter on the front line. If a vendor or someone else arrives to meet with me, I'll stop what I'm doing and conduct the meeting right in the restaurant, not in some executive suite somewhere.

There's the staff dinner at 4:15 p.m., which I usually attend. Afterward, I pop into our back office for an hour or so to do my e-mails. Then our dinner service has started, and I'm back out on the floor, talking to guests and team members, watching what's going on in order to protect and improve upon our brand experience. I usually stick around well into the night, driving home around 10:00 or 10:30 p.m. By then I'm pretty wiped out. I've had a long day of paying attention and a diverse day, too, in which I've dealt with all kinds of unpredictable issues bearing on our operations. The next day, I get up and do it all again, often flying to a different city to work a different restaurant. It's a hands-on style of management that keeps me constantly in the thick of things, in control, and working harder than ever. And it's applicable to owners or leaders in any company, of any size, and in any industry.

I don't mean to suggest that I notice *everything*. Some things do get by me. When I'm in a restaurant during service, I try to check in with guests at most tables, inquiring how they like their experiences. One night during the early 2000s, the restaurant was packed and I was making the usual rounds when the bartender pulled me over. "Steve, this bar guest wants to talk to you."

I went over and introduced myself. The guest wiped his mouth with his napkin and said, "I gotta tell you, I love this restaurant. I come all the time. Best bartenders in the city. The food? I can't believe how good it is. The servers are amazing. But there's one problem."

"Well, what is it?" I asked.

And he said, "You!"

"Wait—me? I'm the problem?"

He nodded. "Yeah! I see you talking to that guy over there, that girl over there, that group over there, that server here. You talk to everybody. But you've never talked to me! You've never *once* come over."

I was shocked. He was right. I never had. "You know what?" I said. "I'm sorry. I messed up. I try to get to everyone, but I missed you."

"You walk right by me! I'm here all the time!"

I pulled up a barstool and sat next to him. We talked together for a half hour. And I told the bartenders to keep an eye out for this guy. It was red alert; the next time he came in, I wanted to know about it. He wound up coming back many times, and each time, no matter what I was doing, I dropped everything to spend a few minutes with him. Sometimes, you need a little help to notice what you should. Even when you're trying as hard as I am. Even when you're Noticer-in-Chief.

⌐⌐

From what I've said so far, you might think that my active management style has me standing over my staff all the time, acting as a policeman. Not true. I do keep a close eye not merely on what team members are saying and doing, how much passion they show, but also on what they're wearing, how many piercings they have, their nails, their shoes. I want them to look the part and fit our brand. At the same time, I tend to serve more as a coach, motivating them, keeping them on their toes, and instructing them on how to do better and reach their potential. I make it my business to be aware of what's going on, and I come prepared with questions. I might approach a bartender and ask, "Hey, Mark, how did it go yesterday?"

"Oh, pretty normal," he'll say.

And then I'll follow up with something like, "We did $7,000 in bar sales. Is that normal?"

As I mentioned in chapter six, I ask these questions to let Mark know that I'm on top of things; that way, he'll feel the need to think about numbers at all times, especially costs. If

I was a celebrity chef who retreated into my kitchen or back office, what incentive would Mark have to pay attention? Instead, I model the kind of passion that I want him to have, and more often than not, he soaks it up himself. Having this kind of conversation also shows Mark that I care about him and his work. It lets him know that he matters, and it inspires him to perform at his best.

I think it's so important to communicate with your people and show them that you care. Not a day goes by when I don't ask questions like these: "How are we doing on labor? What have we got for specials today? Are the Nantucket scallops in? Did they send over good mushrooms today? Any new desserts we're testing out? How many glasses have we been breaking lately?" One day in Atlanta, I went straight to Kathleen, the pastry chef. Georgia peaches were in season, and I couldn't wait to try one. All day long I had been thinking, *Peaches, peaches, peaches!* Kathleen knows how much I love peaches, and so she'd made a new dessert with them: a beautiful Tuscan tart. It was probably the best dessert I'd had in a long time. She was just so excited—and she had someone to share her excitement with. It's that old, "Hey, Mom, watch me!" dynamic. People fly when they know that their work is noticed and appreciated. It's a basic human need.

I try to stay present as a mentor and coach because I remember how much I looked up to people like Bobby Hillson at Seaside. I know that people are more excited to work hard when they admire and connect with the person they're working for. There are many things I *don't* talk about with team members. I try not to ask a lot of personal questions, for fear of having any problems with sexual harassment laws. And I also try not to get too immersed in the disciplinary side of managing people. I leave it to my managers to handle those things as much as possible, because I want to focus on leading by example and being a positive role model for team members.

You might wonder if it's necessary for me to be this involved, now that we have so many experienced and trusted managers in our company. I think it's *more* important! I am always amazed at name-brand chefs or restaurateurs who have achieved some level of success and think, "Wow, I've made it now. I can go to the office and work on the computer and look at numbers all day!" I can't be in every restaurant every day, but I do try to hit one or two. Although I live in Boston, I make it my business to fly down to Atlanta and Philly two or three times a month to spend time in our restaurants there. I try to meet every team member and remember them by name. A lot of big-time chefs have had a restaurant struggle in Atlanta because they thought they could start it up and forget about it. You can't just put your name on a place and think you're done. You have to be there! More to the point, you have to *want* to be there.

Even though I can't physically be everywhere at once, I talk to someone from each of my restaurants almost every day. And thanks to my trusty smartphone, I text and e-mail them, too. I text or call all the team members in our company—almost five hundred, as of this writing—on their birthdays, and our managers give each of them a $50 cash gift. I'm also constantly sending congratulatory e-mails to people who receive kudos from our guests—that, and another $50 cash. Recently, I learned that a bartender of ours in Atlanta had a breast cancer scare. For technical reasons she didn't have health care coverage. I called her personally and told her I would figure something out for her. She was extremely grateful. I relate this not because I'm trying to talk myself up, but simply because this is what I think leaders should do. They should stay in touch with their people, forge and keep a personal bond. This doesn't change when the company gets bigger. You *always* have to be a leader to your people, as much as you possibly can.

What if you don't want to be managing people or keeping an eye on all aspects of operations? What if you *are* just a chef? Should you give up your dream of owning a restaurant? By extension, if you're in another industry and you don't want to stay grounded in the nuts and bolts of your business, should you give up trying to own a company and run the show?

You can still do those things—but you have to have a partner. I do have partners with other businesses I'm involved with, but not with our restaurants. I was fortunate to have gotten training both in business and in cooking, a generalized background that I think any restaurateur should have. Also, I *love* both sides of the restaurant business—the operations and the food. I like being on my own, because that means I get to make the decisions and I don't have to rely on someone else. For all these reasons I've never had a restaurant partner. But if I hadn't had the training, if I had been only to culinary school, if I loved only cooking, I would have wanted to find a partner who really understood business, people, promotions, and the rest of it to handle the bulk of operations. Likewise, if

I was a front-of-house guy who loved only business, I'd team up with a great chef.

Jasper White, a good friend of mine, is probably one of the best chefs in the country. He had his own restaurant for twenty years, but it ran its course. Looking ahead, he realized that he would prefer not to handle the operations side of the business—he is a chef. He wound up reopening with Patrick Lyons and Ed Sparks of the Lyons Group, partners who run twenty-five restaurants in the New England area and *do* get the business side. Jasper and the Lyons group now have five very successful restaurants with Jasper's name on them. Jasper has the freedom to do what he loves to do and let his chef instincts run wild.

It *can't* all be about the chef, or in the case of businesses in general, the big boss. Someone in a business has to get out of the executive suite and work the floor. Someone has to be the operations guy. And that means that someone has to lose the big ego, mingle with the people, and get his hands dirty. It isn't necessarily as glamorous as being a celebrity chef, but you do have the satisfaction of really helping to run something, build something, and make a difference in people's lives, day in and day out.

Some strange things happen when you get your hands dirty. One day back in 1997, I was working the door at Davio's on Newbury Street. We were busy—a forty-five minute wait for a table. A guy came in, an attractive woman by his side. As she looked on he said, "Hey, can you get me a table right now? I know Steve. The owner."

I couldn't believe it. "Oh, you know Steve? Really?"

"Yeah," he said, puffing his chest out. "I'm friends with him. Can you get me in a little sooner?"

I pretended to look down at our list of reservations. "Well, why don't you go upstairs to the bar and let me figure it out, see what I can do?"

I was shocked; I had to get away from the guy to process what was happening. I wasn't about to bump him up in the line, but it turned out that a table opened up quicker than expected, after about only twenty minutes. I found him at the bar. "Sir, I have your table."

The big shot nodded smugly to his girlfriend.

I brought him to the table and sat him down. He looked up at me. "You know what, I'm gonna call Steve tomorrow and tell him that you got me in and how great you are. This is amazing." I swear to God, he said this right to my face.

It didn't occur to this guest that the person at the host stand could actually be the owner. But at Davio's, he often is. Now, most restaurant owners with big egos—whether they are prima donna chefs or not—would have taken the opportunity to embarrass this greaseball in front of his girlfriend. It would have been so easy and so much fun. But I wasn't about to do that. If I had embarrassed him, he would have had a bad time and we never would have seen him again. There was no need for me to score ego points that night. It wasn't about the chef, nor was it about me, the owner. It was about making the sale and running a strong business.

"Sir," I said, "that would be great. I really appreciate it."

Restaurant Lessons to Live By

Don't hide in the kitchen or the boardroom. Get out there and know what your guests need—so that they stick around and have fun.

If you're not in the house keeping an eye on things, your guests will suffer through endless stogies, and your servers will sell veal parm. Is that really what you want?

A fresh Georgia peach, there's nothing like it. Take the time to bond with team members, not merely police their performance.

Put business before ego. Resist the urge to make yourself look good at someone else's expense—even when they most definitely deserve it!

CHAPTER NINE

Restaurants Make a Difference— Wield Your Power!

I've advocated for an active, engaged management style, but that doesn't apply only inside the restaurant; it applies in the wider world, too. Businesses are big players in the communities they serve. They create jobs and contribute to the overall quality of life in a local neighborhood. Restaurants in particular have emotional significance; people rely on us as places where they can celebrate the big events in their life, where they can mark milestones, where they can relax and feel good week in and week out. Given how important your company is, it's vital as owner to be aware of your economic interests and to take action to safeguard them. Even if you wind up ruffling a few feathers along the way.

On second thought, *especially* if you ruffle a few feathers. One of the biggest boosts Davio's ever got didn't come from a marketing decision we made, or a new dish we created, or a new brand extension. It came from publicity we got when I took on an issue that affects most restaurants and businesses: excessive fees charged by credit companies for guest transactions. My involvement in the "Boston Fee Party," as the controversy was called, brought many new guests into Davio's and won me the respect of other restaurateurs.

To develop your business to the fullest, look for opportunities to cooperate with others in your industry. Be vocal about what you need and what you believe to be right. Wield your power. Fight the good fight. And mark my words, good things will follow.

⌁

As lucrative as it turned out to be for us, the Boston Fee Party wasn't intended as a publicity stunt. It wasn't intended as anything. The whole episode sort of snuck up on me in early 1991, not long after we opened our second and third locations in Brookline and Cambridge, respectively. Times were tough for restaurants then. The country was in a recession, people were losing their jobs, and they were eating out less. We saw our lunch business evaporate almost overnight as businesspeople cut back on expenses. Most restaurants like ours responded by going to their vendors and asking to modify contract terms to get a slightly better deal. We went to our garbage guy, for instance, and asked him to come three days a week instead of five and to lower his fee significantly. We did the same with our produce guy, our meat guy—everyone.

Trying to cut costs throughout our operation, we worked through our local bank to approach Visa about lowering its transaction fees. Credit card transactions were becoming automated, a development that made credit card companies more efficient and gave them room to pass savings on to small businesses. Visa was sympathetic and agreed to help us out. At the time, Visa and MasterCard took only about 1.7 percent to 2 percent of every purchase. American Express was the big problem, since it took 3.25 percent—almost double. If you had a small-volume business, you could pay even more, up to 4 percent. It was crazy! I called up American Express, speaking to one of its local representatives. "Your rates are like double what your competition charges," I said. "We're really hurting right now. Any chance you guys can lower the rate?"

"The rates are set by the chairman, and there's nothing I can do about it," the representative said. The chairman was James D. Robinson III, known as a hard-nosed, inflexible business leader. It seemed that we had little hope, if any, of seeing relief. American Express's position seemed so arrogant given that everybody else in the restaurant business was lowering prices. Didn't we matter, too?

A fee of 3.25 percent or more per transaction may not sound like a lot, but for a business doing the kind of volume we were doing, it amounted to tens of thousands of dollars a year. When I did the numbers, I found that I was paying more to American Express than to my landlord. I was getting killed!

A week or two after that call, a number of leading players in the Boston restaurant scene met at Grill 23 to discuss our financial situations. Roger Berkowitz and Kevin Harron from Legal Sea Foods were there, as were Jasper White, Lydia Shire, Chuck Ellis, myself, and some others. Even though we were competitors, we were friendly with one another and enjoyed throwing around ideas. We spent much of that session complaining about American Express and its unwillingness to help out the little guy.

I didn't realize it, but at a nearby table a reporter from the *Boston Herald* was eating lunch. Later that day, he called me up. "Hey, I was at Grill 23 today and saw all you restaurant guys talking. What are you guys up to? You had Jasper, Lydia, Legal Sea Foods—all the big names in the city. Do you guys have a problem with something or somebody?"

I told him that we were all kind of mad at American Express for not lowering its fees. He asked if he could come by to discuss it, and I said, "Sure, no problem."

When he came by the restaurant, I explained our predicament.

"Man, you really don't like American Express," he said.

"Well, everybody else has been willing to work with us, but not them. They've been pretty jerky."

His eyes light up. "Wait! I've got an idea. Would you take your American Express card and chop it up a bit, so I can take a picture?"

I shook my head. "I don't have an American Express card. All I have is a MasterCard or Visa."

He reached into his pocket. "Well, I have one."

I took it from him. "Sure, let's do it. Let's have some fun with it."

We went into the kitchen, and I took a big butcher's knife and rammed it through his card. He snapped a picture of me holding the knife, we talked some more about the recession and how we were coping, and then he left. I went home shortly after, thinking little about it.

The next morning, as I walked down Newbury Street to the restaurant, I noticed lots of trucks parked up ahead. They had these huge satellite dishes on their roofs, and the machinery they were running was loud. As I got closer I saw that they were news trucks: Channel 5, Channel 7. *Uh-oh, there must have been a murder here,* I thought.

Then I realized that the trucks were in front of Davio's. What in the world could be going on? Today, people would have texted and tweeted the news, but back then, before cell phones, I had no idea.

I reached the restaurant, going down the stairs to the front door, and greeted a bunch of people standing around. "What's going on here?" I asked.

A guy said, "Great shot in the *Herald* today. Do you mind speaking on camera about it?"

"What picture? What *Herald*?"

"You don't know?" He held up the newspaper. "What do you think about this?"

I took a look and nearly lost it. What did I do? My PR representative was going to kill me! This couldn't be good.

Feeling that I had no choice, that I had to roll with it, I talked to the reporters there and to others who called me up as the day went on. My PR representative, Dee Dee Cheraton, did in fact want to kill me. "Are you crazy, Steve?" she asked when she called me. Nevertheless, she coached me on what to say and what to avoid. I must have told the story fifty times that day. American Express was a huge, multibillion dollar company, and the idea that a little guy like me was taking them on publicly—going so far as to stick a knife through the card—seemed pretty outrageous. Who the hell was I to be doing this? And yet, there I was.

The story took on a momentum of its own. The next morning, my dad called me. "Steve, I'm on my way to Florida. Are you aware that you're on the front page of the *Wall Street Journal?*"

Lo and behold I was, and I was on the cover of the *Boston Globe,* too. Later that day, CNN called me for an interview. I was on every radio show. Someone told me that Robinson, American Express's chairman, freaked out upon seeing the *Boston Herald* with my picture on it, saying, "Who is this fucking asshole up in Boston?" I can only imagine what he thought over the next couple of weeks when *Newsweek* and *Time* ran stories on me. Remember, this was before the Internet and media fragmentation, so getting in those magazines was a big deal. It was a national story; *everyone* was talking about it.

In retrospect, I think that some of this publicity was a little misplaced. Some restaurants in Boston and around the country stopped accepting American Express. I never said I would do that. I didn't think it was fair to pull the plug before we had sat down with American Express to try to work this out. If we could get the company to negotiate, I didn't see a need to stop accepting its card.

Somehow, none of this mattered, and I became known as the leader of the Boston-based revolt against American Express. I was in the papers for days. We had tapped into something; the press reported that as many as one hundred restaurants were joining our cause and potentially dropping American Express if it didn't lower its outrageous fees. I had people from Canada calling me, and a guy from Indianapolis flew in to talk to me about joining the revolt. In *Setting the Table,* one of my favorite books of all time, Danny Meyer—at the time the best-known restaurateur in New York—recalled thinking about joining up with us to pressure American

Express. In the end he didn't, following his father's advice that this was my fight, not Danny's. That long upset me (although I'm over it now, and when we see each other, we joke about it).

The whole episode lasted about six to eight weeks. I was so consumed with it that I felt I was barely working in the restaurant. My days were filled with press interviews and meetings with other restaurateurs whom we were trying to have join us in the revolt. There were negotiations, too. After a week I got a call from our local American Express representative saying that Don Karlin, a big New York executive with the company, would come meet with us. That meeting didn't go well; Karlin didn't take us seriously or seem willing to make any concessions. We left the meeting even angrier than before and determined to stand our ground.

A week later, as the controversy mushroomed across the country, American Express finally got serious and sent another representative, Mike Mancuso, who was less hard-nosed and more willing to listen to our concerns. After another five to six weeks of meetings, we had a deal. Restaurants with $1 million in American Express charges would pay 2.95 percent, and American Express also agreed to fund a marketing campaign in the Boston area to convince people to eat out more. The rate still wasn't as low as the other credit card companies charged, but it was low enough to save us thousands of dollars. We had won.

It was crazy after that; I didn't have to pay for a single meal in Boston for a year! Everywhere I went to eat, owners approached me and said, "Steve, thank you so much!" Lots of people love an underdog, and an underdog I was. My fifteen minutes of fame was a little scary at first, and it took up a lot of my time, but it ultimately benefitted us. Guests from all around the country would visit Boston and come to Davio's because they had heard of us. We got additional publicity on the tenth and twentieth anniversaries of the event. Even today, you can go online and find articles about what happened. Every once in a while, someone will still come up to me and joke, "Hey, you taking American Express these days?"

I am glad for all that, but I was also glad I had seized an opportunity to stand up for something I believed in. What American Express was doing to small businesses like mine was just *wrong*. Someone had to say something, and I guess that person turned out to be me. I have always wondered about those few restaurants that didn't join us. Did they pay the old, higher rates or the new one?

I got a good laugh a month or two after the settlement was announced. We were holding a big gala for the Spinazzola Foundation, the Boston-area charity I told you about in chapter seven. Today, you see many charities around the country holding tasting events, but this was one of the first, and it was big—at least four thousand people in attendance, with invited chefs from around the country. As part of the event, we held a raffle, and American Express, in an effort to mend fences with us, had donated $500 in gift cards as a door prize. At one point in the evening, I looked up at the stage and saw Don Karlin standing there at the microphone. He and I had butted heads a lot during the negotiations, and although he had made nice, it was clear he didn't like me. "Steve DiFillippo, get over here," he said.

I didn't understand what was going on. What? Why would Don Karlin be calling me up?

Someone nearby said, "Steve, you won! $500 in gift cards."

And so there was the big-shot American Express guy, handing little old me a prize. Out of four thousand people in the room. What were the chances of that happening?

I went on stage, claimed my prize, and shook his hand for the camera. I think it's safe to say that his smile was not as big as mine. Pretty sweet!

Warm Chocolate Cake
(for When You Want to Celebrate)

It's easy to forget to preheat the oven, so make sure to do that first. A full 375°F, with a high fan on. Now, take 12 ½-cup aluminum tins and coat well with nonstick spray and flour. Grab a **9½-ounce bag bittersweet chocolate** (I use 60/40 Callebaut) and pour it into a mixing bowl—we'll need this in just a second. Melt **10½ ounces unsalted butter** and pour it over that chocolate to melt it. In another large mixing bowl, sift **5¼ ounces pastry flour** and **10½ ounces confectioners sugar** together. Add in **6 whole eggs** and **6 egg yolks** and mix until smooth. Then combine the flour/sugar bowl with the chocolate/butter bowl—stir and stir until they're homogeneous. Deposit this chocolaty goodness into the prepared tins and then put the tins into the oven. Bake approximately 10 minutes or until the outside edges are set. When you remove the cakes from the oven, let them sit briefly so they unmold on their own.

Today, I'm happy to say that American Express and I are great friends. The company has become a strong partner for us and other restaurants, donating millions of dollars to food-related causes. Nobody else even comes close to what it's done over the last twenty years. It sponsors restaurant weeks in many cities and helps with marketing for individual restaurants. It's done more for us than it ever said it would do back in 1991 during our negotiations. In fact, the restaurant business wouldn't be as vibrant as it is today were it not for American Express. The company's current chairman, Ken Chenault, also lives in New England and dines regularly at Davio's. He's had birthday celebrations with us and a dinner for his son's Harvard graduation. I'm proud that we've been able to move beyond past differences and build a strong partnership. It's too bad he wasn't CEO twenty years ago. If he had been, the Boston Fee Party never would have happened.

In the aftermath of the Boston Fee Party, I stayed in touch with restaurant issues, becoming involved in the Massachusetts Restaurant Association. I also made friends with a number of political and business leaders in the markets we serve, and supported other groups such as the Anti-Defamation League. Yet by and large I stayed out of the political limelight, until another burning business-related issue brought me back in, this time at the state level.

For years pharmaceutical companies had sponsored private lunches and dinners at restaurants, using them as occasions to educate doctors about new drugs. Some doctors and others in the medical community didn't like this marketing technique; it seemed to give drug companies too much influence over what doctors prescribed. In 2009 the Massachusetts legislature enacted a wide-ranging law regulating pharmaceutical companies. Among many other things, the law banned companies from holding educational dinners or lunches at restaurants. If you've been to Boston, you know how many large, world-renowned medical institutions there are. We have a *lot* of doctors in town, and those educational lunches and dinners had become a big business for us. Overnight, the "pharma ban," as it was called, wiped out 20 percent of our private function business, and it hit many other restaurants in our state just as much. I'm talking more than $1 million in annual revenue for us alone, just *gone.*

It wasn't just owners like me who were hit hard. Servers lost a substantial portion of their income, as did our salespeople and practically everyone else who worked for us. This negative effect reverberated around the larger economy; restaurants are the second-largest employer in the state, and now our staff couldn't afford to spend as much money on the everyday things they needed for their households. My server Tonino, who was painting his house, couldn't afford painters any longer; he had to do it himself. Sales manager Patty LaBella, whom I told you about in chapter five, was sending her son to college; now she needed to take out a larger loan. Our chef Eric couldn't buy a new car any longer; he had to buy a used car. And these stories went on and on.

I was devastated and didn't know what to do about it. I talked to people I knew about trying to get the law changed, but everyone seemed to think this unlikely. Members of the health care community were strongly opposed to the ways that drug companies marketed their products; they weren't in the mood to make exceptions for restaurants. "Steve, you're wasting your time," a friend of mine who worked for Pfizer said.

At a Christmas party for my PR firm, Regan Communications, I ended up meeting the president of the Massachusetts Senate, Therese Murray, who unbeknownst to me had written the pharma ban. We made small talk for a little while, and then I left to attend another party in Boston's North End for a charity I'm involved with. I was there not even twenty minutes when who should stroll in but Therese Murray again. I approached her. "You know, I've always wanted to meet you, and here it is, twice in one night!" She laughed and we talked a little more. That night, as I was driving home, I said to myself, "You know, I wonder if she could help us with this pharma thing."

I called the state senate the next day and asked to speak to her. "This is Steve from Davio's. I'd like to meet with Senator Murray. I've got something I'd like to discuss."

The lady on the phone said, "Sir, you can't just *call* the state senate president and come see her—are you kidding me?"

"Why not? I'm a taxpayer. I'm a state resident. I need to discuss some issues with her."

"Okay, well, you'll need to contact the person who schedules her appointments, and they'll get back to you."

I e-mailed this person. When do you think I heard from her? Well, I'm still waiting for an answer.

After six weeks I became really frustrated, so I called up the head of the Massachusetts Restaurant Association, Peter

Christie. I explained why I wanted to talk to Therese Murray and related how difficult it was to get a meeting. "Steve, welcome to my world," Christie said. "I will try my best to get you a meeting."

Christie managed to arrange a meeting with myself, celebrity chef and restaurateur Ming Tsai, restaurateur Bill Brady, lobbyists Bill Coyne and Tricia McCarthy, some legislative aides, and Senator Murray. As we sat in the senator's office in the State House, I explained how the bill was devastating our business.

"What do you mean?" she asked. "I don't understand. I thought you were still able to have these pharma educational sessions in your restaurants."

"No, we can't." The law banned these events from taking place in restaurants, but pharma companies could still hold them in hospitals. Senator Murray didn't realize this and said she would look into it. In the meantime, she advised us to talk to some other senators and see what they thought.

I did that. Out of the forty state senators in Massachusetts, Bill Coyne, Tricia McCarthy, and I must have met with thirty of them. For two months I went almost every week to meet with two or three senators. Some of them, such as Dick Moore and Mark Montigny, disagreed with me, saying that the senate would never overturn even a part of the law regulating pharma companies. When I relayed how much money the servers, cooks, salespeople and other workers in our industry were losing, they said things like, "That's good, Steve. That means the law is working." Still, I did everything I could to convince them. I worked really hard on this. I had no choice: The law was hurting my business and our industry that much.

We managed to have the senate draft a new bill that reinstated pharma events in restaurants. It was put to a vote. We needed twenty-one senators to support the measure for it to pass. We were convinced that we had the votes, but much to our disappointment, we lost. Only eighteen senators supported us.

I discovered which of the senators had turned on us, and I went to see one of them. "What happened?" I asked the man. "You were right there saying this ban doesn't make sense and is needlessly hurting restaurants. Why did you change your vote?"

The senator said, "Well, Steve, senate leadership is very important to me, and when they don't want something to go through, we can't vote it in. I had to change my vote. I'm sorry."

It didn't seem like there was much we could do. I was crushed. I had spent so much time lobbying for support, and I had failed.

I couldn't give up, though. My team members were depending on me. Not a day went by when one of them didn't come up to me and ask how my lobbying effort was going. This was in 2010, when the economy was still recovering from the Great Recession. Restaurant business was bad all around. We needed a break. And it was extremely frustrating to see our restaurants in Philly and Atlanta booming with educational medical dinners while in Boston we were struggling.

The following year, I again tried to get the senate to rescind the ban, which was even harder since the senators knew that a number of their leaders wanted the ban in place. The other legislative body, the Massachusetts House of Representatives, was on our side, but Speaker of the House Bob DeLeo wanted the *entire* law regulating pharma companies abolished, not just the little part we cared about that affected restaurants.

This wound up hurting us, since it was harder for the senators to vote to overturn the entire law as opposed to just one line. We were handed another defeat.

I still hadn't given up. In 2011 I embarked on an all-out grassroots effort to convince senate leaders to help us out. Joined by Bill Coyne and Tricia McCarthy, I spoke to dozens of prominent business and community leaders. I would have talked to my mailman about the issue if I could! I felt like I needed to keep the momentum going at all times. Anthony Petruccelli, a Democratic state senator whom I had rallied to my cause, also spoke on our behalf to numerous political figures in the state. As I explained to everyone I met, I didn't care about overturning the entire law, just the little sentence that applied to restaurants. It wasn't fair that hospitals could still hold these educational lunches and dinners in-house, but not in restaurants. What were we, second-class citizens?

One day in early 2012, senate leadership called Bill Coyne and said that they were willing to meet with me again. A number of us sat down together: Jim Carmody (general manager of the Seaport Hotel), Senator Murray, Senator Petruccelli, Senator Moore and his staff, myself, and some others. At the beginning of the session, Senator Murray said, "I've been rethinking this law and I've decided we need to do something for the restaurant community."

I almost fell off my chair.

Senator Petruccelli then defended the restaurant community, talking about how we were large employers and that many people in our state were being hurt by the pharma ban. Senator Moore, who had been so against lifting the ban, said that he would no longer oppose a change in the law, so long as there was adequate transparency about what the drug companies were doing. When the meeting adjourned it seemed that we had finally achieved the necessary consensus to get the pharma ban changed.

Six months after that meeting, the house voted to rescind the ban, and we now had thirty votes in the senate behind us to get the law rewritten in our favor. Senate leaders allowed the law to reach the desk of the governor, Deval Patrick. I thought we were all set. All along, I had been talking to the governor, and he had told me, "Steve, if you can send the bill getting rid of the ban to my desk, I'll sign it." But I hadn't counted on how strong the opposition would be from the health care community. Shortly before the governor was supposed to sign, a lobbyist for the Restaurant Association called. "Steve, I don't know if the governor's going to sign it. He's taking some really strong heat."

In the end he did sign. Afterward, I talked to him about it, and he told me he was always going to sign. "Steve, I gave you my word, and I thought that it was the right thing to do. Restaurants are important, and we need to support them."

I just love Governor Patrick. He kept his word. And I will forever be grateful to Senator Petruccelli, who never gave up fighting for us.

Fighting the pharma ban was tough, but I'm so glad I stayed the course. It was one of the best things I've ever done for my business and the restaurant community. The ban was not just hurting restaurants like mine that hosted pharma events; it hurt everyone. When all these events got cancelled, people like me were forced to open our private function rooms to a la carte dining, which meant we were taking guests who would otherwise have gone to other restaurants because they couldn't get a table with us.

Some restaurateurs aren't thinking about the larger picture—the community. They're only thinking about their own place. That's a big mistake. We all rise and fall together. Today, thanks to the lifting of the ban, our private function business is thriving in Massachusetts, and the overall restaurant scene is much healthier than it would have been.

_____

Although it is important to have a voice, I'm not suggesting that restaurateurs should make it their business to get involved in every fight, nor do I think they should identify with a particular political group or party. I mean, if that's your thing, go crazy. But if you want to do what's best for business, then do what I do and cultivate neutrality. I make sure to remain publicly uncommitted in terms of my political affiliation. I have good friends on both the Democrat and Republican sides (and keep in mind, Massachusetts, where I'm based, is a pretty blue state). As I always say, I'm like Switzerland in the business community. I stay engaged—but neutral.

I got the whole Switzerland thing from my family, especially my grandmother, Nana. She was the original Switzerland. For an old lady she was surprisingly open-minded and tolerant, cultivating a "live and let live" attitude. Let me close this chapter with a story. When I became old enough to drive, it was my job to pick up Nana and Papa in Providence and take them to our house in Lynnfield, Massachusetts, for the Thanksgiving holiday. During my sophomore year at Boston University, I brought home one of my roommates, an African-American student on the football team named Alex, for the holiday weekend. My parents were pretty freaked out about how Nana would react. None of us had ever brought an African American to a family event before. "When you go down there," my mother said, "make sure you tell Nana that Alex is coming for dinner. We don't want him to just walk on in and surprise her."

I went down to pick my grandparents up. As usual we stopped at Venda Ravioli, the Colonial Market, and a couple of other places to pick up food. The car smelled great with all the home-cooked Italian specialties Nana had bought. (I later learned to put our purchases in the trunk; I was always hungry, and the smell of that food was killing me.) Nana sat in the front seat, Papa in back. I spent the entire hour-and-a-half-long drive up to Lynnfield trying unsuccessfully to tell her about Alex. I didn't know what to say, but like my mother, I was afraid Nana would be unfriendly to Alex and make him uncomfortable.

I finally pulled up to our street, Cider Mill Road. "Whatever you do," my mother had said, "you make sure you tell her before you get out of that car." It was getting close. Alex was staying at our house. As soon as Nana got there, she would see him.

I broke out into a sweat and almost missed my driveway, I was so nervous. "Nana," I said, bringing the car to a stop, "by the way, I just want you to know that my roommate from college is going to be here. He's staying with us for Thanksgiving because he lives in Chicago."

She smiled. "Oh, that's great. What's his name?"

"Alexander Reed."

"Oh, great. I'm looking forward to meeting him."

I cleared my throat. "Well, just so you know, he's on the football team. He's really good, a defensive end, really fast."

"That's nice. Great that he plays football."

"Well, he's also African American. I just thought you'd want to know."

She looked at me funny, and in her strong Italian accent she said, "What do you mean? You mean he's black?"

I couldn't help but laugh. "Yeah."

She waved me off. "Oh, Stevie, whatever. Why do I care? He sounds like a great guy. I don't care what color he is. I can't wait to meet him."

"Really?"

"Sure. What's the big deal?"

I couldn't believe it. I felt so relieved, I almost started to cry. This issue that I had gotten so nervous about turned out to be nothing. Black, blue—my Nana didn't care. I developed a whole new respect for her that day. People were people in her book. We shouldn't judge. And that's the spirit that I bring to all my business dealings, and specifically to any political differences people might have. It's so important as a restaurateur to fight for what you believe in. Speaking out can have all kinds of positive consequences, including publicity, a chance to cultivate relationships with powerful people, and most of all, the satisfaction that comes from banding together with other members of your community to get the job done. But never go over the line and take sides where you don't need to. It's just not your role, and it's bad for business. Why alienate a whole pool of potential guests?

Switzerland—taught to me by a little old woman from Italy.

Restaurant Lessons to Live By

Speak out, stand up, raise your hand. Stirring the pot can benefit you in ways you never imagined.

Keep it real. Don't look for publicity. If you wind up on the cover of the Wall Street Journal, *great, but fight for a cause you really believe in.*

If you really believe in something, stick with it. I spent three years fighting the pharma ban—and today, when I see my private function rooms filled, I know it was worth it.

My nana didn't take sides, and neither should you. Do what I do: Eat Northern Italian, but behave like Switzerland.

CHAPTER TEN

Stay Fresh or Die

Let's say you've worked hard and built up a successful business. My advice to you: Change what you're doing!

What!? Why?

Because every business has a shelf life. How many times can guests go back to the same restaurant, even one they love? How many times can they go back to the same website, pharmacy, barbershop? Eventually they get sick of it, or their needs change, and they seek out other options. That's just the way life is—especially these days, with markets and technology changing faster than ever. If you want to stay in business, you constantly have to update and improve what you're doing. Sometimes, you have to go further and *blow the whole thing up.*

There's a restaurant in Hamilton, Massachusetts, called the Black Cow that was thriving during the '90s—packed every night. By the mid-2000s it had lost its mojo. Chef after chef left, then the best servers. The decor was dated and dirty. Other, hipper restaurants opened up in the local community. So what did the owner, Joe Leone, do? He blew it up! One day, he closed it and completely renovated it. Knocked a wall down, creating one huge space. Doubled the bar seats. Installed a fireplace. Hired a new chef and servers. I have to think he spent $500,000 on the renovations. The whole restaurant is different. And now, you can't get into the place again. It's packed night after night.

In 2002 I did something similar and blew up my original Davio's concept. Thank God, too, because it launched us onto a whole new level of success. I had owned my little restaurant on Newbury Street for seventeen years, was running a Davio's in Providence, Rhode Island (more on that later), and by this time also owned a Davio's in Philly (more on that soon, too) and a fourth in Cambridge. All our restaurants were making money, but sales at Newbury Street had dropped from their peak of $3.5 million to about $2 million a year. Lunches were slow; the place in general had lost excitement. We needed to do something big to refresh the menu, but our options were limited. Our kitchen was cramped, and there was no room in our four-thousand-square-foot space to expand it. Wanting to grow our brand into a much bigger company, I didn't feel a small restaurant like this was going to cut it any longer; it wasn't part of our vision.

Our lease was coming up for renewal, and the landlord and I didn't get along very well, so I realized we needed to move. We were fortunate to find a space six blocks away, on Arlington Street. The place was much bigger—nine thousand square feet—which would change everything. Our menu would be twice the size and feature steakhouse items as well as the Northern Italian specialties our Newbury Street patrons loved. In fact, we wouldn't be a "Northern Italian

Restaurant" any longer—we would be a "Northern Italian Steakhouse." Our dining room would seat as many as 130 (as compared to 80 at Newbury Street), and we would have private function rooms seating an additional 130. Our bar would seat twenty-eight instead of five. The decor would be sleek, modern, upscale, and sophisticated, with high ceilings, hardwood floors, and an open kitchen—a far cry from the brick walls, curtains, and homey feel of the original Davio's. Newbury Street worked great during the '80s; Arlington was a restaurant for the twenty-first century.

In the weeks leading up to the grand opening, I barely slept or saw my family. I was working as hard as I could to make the new Davio's a success. I felt excited—but nervous. I had put $2.8 million into the build-out, stretching to afford the investment. I had tried the "Northern Italian Steakhouse" concept out in Philadelphia, and it had worked, but I didn't know if it would succeed in Boston. Our regulars liked the traditional food and the small, intimate space we had on Newbury Street. Would they move with us to Arlington? If they didn't, would we attract a new clientele? And then there were operational questions. How would we handle the new volume?

Turned out I had nothing to worry about. We were packed in Arlington from day one. The *Boston Globe* gave us a fantastic review, helping us even more. Our Friday and Saturday night seatings were booked weeks in advance. Although we initially had trouble handling the volume (leading to the train wreck of an evening that I described in an earlier chapter), we added more staff and made other adjustments, and that took care of the problem. I worked so hard those first few months, running server stations, helping out in the kitchen, and greeting guests at the door. When some of our old guests asked me if I missed my quaint little restaurant on Newbury Street, I pointed to all the full tables. "What do you think?" Some regulars gradually dwindled away, replaced by a new clientele of people who loved prime steak and were willing to pay for it. The numbers we did were amazing. We were bringing in more sales in one day than we had done in an entire *week* at Newbury Street! We went from $2 million in sales to $8 million the first year.

A couple of weeks before we reopened, longtime Boston television news anchor Natalie Jacobson dropped by our new location. The place was still a mess; workers were finishing the floor, and we had not yet installed tables or chairs or finished the walls. I was excited to see her and showed her where everything would be when we were done. "Wow, great," she said. "Good luck." She seemed happy for us, but something about the way she reacted was weird. I couldn't quite place it.

A month later, when we were open, she came in for dinner. The place was packed—absolutely nuts. She gave me a big hug, and tears formed in her eyes.

"Natalie, what's wrong?"

She smiled through her tears. "Steve, you have no idea how I felt when I came in here last time. I thought you were going to lose everything. I thought you were out of your mind, building this enormous restaurant." She looked around. "I just can't believe what you've done here. It's such a huge difference from Newbury Street."

I can understand Natalie's initial impression. The fact is that many successful restaurateurs shrink from remaking themselves so dramatically. They are afraid to take that kind of risk, and they don't want to put in that kind of effort. When they see sales stagnating, they grope for some small tactic to save the day. They try an advertising campaign, do a coupon promotion, run a two-for-one special, make a few small adjustments to the menu. Maybe they see a short bump, but then sales return to the same disappointing levels. Here's the thing: One good Saturday night is not going to save a stale restaurant. Restaurants go out of business because their owners don't alter the formula when they still have a chance. Have you been to a Bennigan's lately, or a Perkin's pancake restaurant? Didn't think so.

Don't think that what once made you successful will *always* make you successful. Embrace change. Do what it takes in order to stay fresh. If you don't stay fresh, you will die—much faster than you ever thought possible.

Now, I will be the first to admit, turning a proven but tired $2 million restaurant into a booming $8 million restaurant isn't easy. An owner certainly can't do it alone. In the back of the house at Arlington, we had three longtime chefs who knew Davio's inside and out: Eric, Steve, and Rodney. Joining them was Tom Ponticelli, a pastry chef who had formerly worked at the Four Seasons and who was helping us dramatically improve our desserts. In the front of the house, we had myself, Joanie Raphael, and Eleanor Arpino. Joanie had been my boss at Seaside years earlier when I worked as a busser. In 2002, when Bobby Hillson sold his restaurant, she came to work with me—seventeen years after we had first worked together! She served as our invaluable daytime manager on Arlington Street. Eleanor, meanwhile, was a real pro whom we had hired first as a consultant to coach our servers and then as general manager of Cambridge. She was by my side the entire time, running everything in the back of the house, including the numbers. She helped take our service to a whole new level. With both Eleanor and Joanie there, I was freed up to be the face of the restaurant. I spent hour after hour touching every table and making sure every guest was happy. The three of us together were an amazing team. You can't run a company like mine without having a number of trusted team members like Eleanor and Joanie.

We also pulled off our astonishing growth because we were already in the habit of thinking creatively. As I've mentioned, the Northern Italian steakhouse concept had been trial tested in a different market by the time we reopened on Arlington Street. I had long been verging beyond the confines of what I was already doing, dreaming up new ideas, imagining the next restaurant, and the one after that. I had long been asking, "What if?" And I had been seizing important opportunities to branch out into new territories.

In 1998 I had gotten a phone call from Mike Feldott, a restaurant broker down in Texas who specializes in putting independent restaurants in hotels. We were already in the Royal Sonesta in Cambridge and had been in the Biltmore in Providence. "Hey, Steve," Mike said, "I've got a space in Philly you should look at. It's going to be in a new Club Quarters hotel. Why don't you come down and check it out?"

Philly didn't sound so hot to me. When I was in college, I was going to stop there on my way driving to California, but my father told me not to; he was afraid of race riots in the city. Of course, that made my pal Supy and I want to go even more. A riot? How cool! We stopped and were surprised to find that not only was there no action in Philadelphia, but there were very few tall buildings—or good restaurants. The impression of Philly as a small, sleepy city had stayed with me all these years. But I went down anyway to meet with Ralph Bahna and John Horowitz, owners of the new Club Quarters. As my plane made its approach into the airport, I was surprised to see a lot of skyscrapers. Boy, had I been wrong. The city was busy and thriving—I couldn't believe the transformation! It was so impressive.

The restaurant space itself was amazing. It was located right near Rittenhouse Square and the main Center City district, where all the tall buildings were, in the stately old Provident Bank building. The space, which was being completely renovated, had tall ceilings, massive windows, and a huge private room on the top floor with an outdoor patio overlooking the city of Philadelphia. I could see a beautiful restaurant opening up there.

As I was inspecting the space with Steve Todisco, our restaurant designer, I looked out the window and saw a man run out of Daffy's clothing store across the street. Two guys ran after him, jumped on him, and cuffed him. Almost immediately, a police wagon pulled up; they threw the guy in, and the wagon drove off. All this took place inside of thirty seconds. It was the craziest thing I'd ever seen. Steve turned to me. "So you want to open a restaurant here, huh?"

Yes, I did. Besides loving the space and being impressed by Philadelphia's growth, I hit it off with Ralph and John, and they offered me a great lease. I thought we could make a go of it. The question became what kind of restaurant to put in. I already had a gem of an answer. In Boston, Grill 23 was my favorite restaurant, and I was always impressed by how successful it was. Some guests at fine-dining establishments didn't want a fully plated entrée; they just wanted a high-quality piece of meat or fish, maybe a side of something, like they got at a steakhouse. I would run into guys who worked at Grill 23 and they would say, "Yeah, we did $50,000 tonight." $50,000!? How the hell did they do that? On Newbury Street we did $10,000 on a night when we were jammed. I was jealous, but I also thought, *Good for them!*

I spent a few days doing market research in Philadelphia, walking around the city and visiting restaurants, seeing what they had and didn't have. Like Boston, they had plenty of great Italian restaurants, especially in South Philly, which is like Boston's North End or Providence's Federal Hill. But Philadelphia's Center City district hardly had any fine steakhouses—just a Morton's and a Palm, as far as I could tell. What if I brought a Grill 23–type steakhouse to Philadelphia and Italianized it? We could brand it as Davio's without any problem, because nobody in the local area was familiar with the original Davio's concept. And the space I was looking at was perfect for a steakhouse—high ceilings, masculine, a feeling of substance and weight.

I knew I couldn't do it alone. I was fortunate enough to hire Shawn Sollberger as chef and Ettore Ceraso as general manager. Shawn had worked as a chef at Morton's as well as at an upscale Italian restaurant called Sfuzzi—if anyone would get the fusion concept I was thinking about, he would.

Ettore had grown up in an Italian family like me and had run the dining room at the Four Seasons, one of Philadelphia's finest restaurants. The three of us sat down together and fleshed out exactly what a Northern Italian steakhouse menu would look like. We took the best and most popular of the fully plated entrées, pastas, salads, and appetizers on the original Davio's Northern Italian menu and combined that with the kinds of meat, fish, and sides offered a la carte at a traditional steakhouse. Our menu size doubled from fifty to a hundred items. Diners in Philadelphia could now get the best of both concepts—the finest steaks *and* exquisitely prepared traditional Italian recipes—all in one place.

The new Davio's concept in Philadelphia was an instant success. The launch went well, critics loved it, and we became a hot dining destination. We grossed $4 million the first year—double what Newbury Street was doing at the time. But not everybody was sold on the concept; Italians sometimes came up to me and said that there was no such thing as a Northern Italian steakhouse. They were totally right! People don't eat a lot of steak in Northern Italy. But as I told them, I don't live in Italy. I live in America, and here we make stuff up!

The new menu made Davio's more diverse and capable of appealing to a broader group of diners. Italian food can be heavy, loaded down with carbs; now people who were more health conscious could come to Davio's and order a piece of grilled salmon and a side of asparagus and be happy. The new menu also gave guests much more choice. Instead of one kind of steak and a couple of seafood dishes, we were now offering ten different kinds of each. At the original Davio's we had not offered side orders; now we had a whole section. Some food critics don't like big menus, preferring that restaurants focus on a few core items; I say, why can't we do lots of things and excel at them all?

The new Davio's on Arlington Street, then, was a logical extension of previous efforts to update and innovate. I didn't do it all at once or in an impulsive way. Even the location on Arlington Street—which ironically enough was just down the block from Grill 23—had been in the works for some time. Years earlier, it had been a furniture store. My wife and I had been in there looking for a bureau or something, and I had said to her, "Pam, wouldn't this be a great restaurant?"

I remember that she ignored me. I say something like this almost everywhere we go. If I opened a restaurant every time I said that, I'd have restaurants all over the world.

Just after 9/11, as I was planning our exit from Newbury Street, I heard that a couple of big Boston restaurant guys, Michael Schlow and Chris Meyers, were planning on putting a restaurant in the furniture store space. I was friends with them both and didn't want to get in their way. I called up Emily Ou, a broker who was involved with that property, and told her to call me if the deal with those two guys ever fell through. "Realistically," she said, "I don't think that's ever going to happen."

But it did happen. Months later, I was attending a fundraiser at a well-known Boston restaurant, Abe & Louie's. I was walking down the stairs, standing on a landing, when I got the call. "Steve," Emily said, "the deal is dead."

"Which deal?"

"For Arlington Street. But Tony Pangaro [the owner of the building] wants to meet with you tomorrow at 9:00 a.m. to hear what you want to do with the space. You better be prepared."

I was shocked. "Emily, you're giving me no time. How can I be prepared?"

"You've got all night to think about it."

I immediately called Steve Todisco and told him to meet me over at Arlington. Actually, before I called Steve, I called my wife and said, "Hey, you won't believe this. Remember that old furniture store on Arlington Street? That could be the next Davio's!" I was so excited.

"Here we go again," she replied. I'd made these announcements to her so many times that she was understandably skeptical.

Anyhow, I told Steve I wanted to take our Philadelphia concept even further. This Arlington Street space was big and open—could we have an open kitchen? Steve liked that idea and suggested a big, circular bar in the shape of a boat, since he's big into boats. We sketched it all out, and the next day, Tony Pangaro loved it—so much that we were eventually able to negotiate an attractive lease, including substantial money from Tony for a build-out.

And like that, the main elements of the new, updated, bigger, more profitable Davio's were in place. I will always remember the moment when I got Emily's call. It seemed to mark a turning point in my life. To this day, when I'm in Abe & Louie's, I sometimes look at that staircase landing and smile.

A number of points embedded in the larger story of the New Davio's are worth elaborating on. The first is pretty simple: Be bold! As an entrepreneur you want to be smart about the risks you take, but there are times in business when you just have to put your money on the table and take the plunge.

As big a financial risk that Arlington was, there have been other moments when I've gone even farther beyond my comfort zone. After we opened on Arlington, New England Patriots owner Robert Kraft and his son Jonathan became regulars. Jonathan even honored us by celebrating his fortieth birthday there. We became good friends. In 2006 Robert first floated the idea of having me open a Davio's Northern Italian Steakhouse at Patriot Place, a new lifestyle center he was opening next to Gillette Stadium, where the Patriots play. "You mean a mall?" I asked.

"No, a lifestyle center."

"What's the difference?"

"Trust me. It's different."

I liked the Krafts and wanted to do business with them, but I just couldn't imagine a restaurant there. Foxboro is way out in the Boston suburbs, and at the time there was nothing out there besides the stadium. Davio's had always been an urban concept. Would guests in the suburbs really want to spend as much for a nice dinner as guests in Boston did? People usually came to the city to spend money, not the other way around. And was a lifestyle center really that different from a mall? I didn't want Davio's to be a "mall restaurant." That had a certain stigma, bringing to mind more generic chain restaurants that were different from our brand. I was also really hesitant given our history in Brookline. We been unable to get suburban guests there to spend the kind of money we needed in order to stay profitable.

I didn't tell the Krafts no, because I valued them so much as guests and as people; I didn't want to insult them. But I didn't tell them yes, either. One day, after the idea had come up several times, Jonathan called me. "Steve, why don't you come to the stadium? I just want to show you the model and plans for the center. Just come down and take a look." I went out there, and Jonathan showed me around. I'm a huge football fan, and it was so amazing to meet the players and to see trophies, footballs, old helmets, and other memorabilia collected on shelves and mounted on walls. It was like the Hard Rock Cafe on steroids! We went into the bowels of the stadium and visited the running backs' room, where the athletes sit in huge chairs to watch tapes of their performances. The whole thing was surreal to me. Jonathan knew what a fan I was, and I had to think he was trying to impress me. Jonathan Kraft, trying to impress me? How cool was that!

We sat down and he showed me the plan. I was impressed. This did not look like an ordinary mall. It *was* a lifestyle center, with over a million square feet of great shopping and other attractions. And of course the stadium was right there. "What's it going to take to get you to come out here? You're our favorite restaurant," Jonathan said. "We really want you here." I told him that I would need rent to be pegged at a certain level, and I would need a certain amount of help with the build-out. I wasn't trying to negotiate; I was just giving him an honest, ballpark assessment of what the financials looked like for me.

"Okay," he said. "No problem. Anything else?" When I told him there wasn't he put out his hand. "It's a done deal. Let's go have lunch." We shook, and like that, after literally thirty seconds of conversation, Davio's was coming to Patriot Place.

I ultimately wound up making the move despite my reservations because given the numbers we were talking about, I thought it was worth a chance. "Who knows?" I said. "Maybe Davio's can make it in a suburban development. Wouldn't that be cool?" Jonathan was talking about bringing other big local restaurants in as tenants, and in fact they did come. It turned out to be a great deal for all of us. Our Patriot Place restaurant today is humming, especially during dinner. All the restaurants in the lifestyle center perform well; the location has become a nightlife and entertainment magnet for people in the area, saving them the long drive or train ride into Boston. Also, about 40 percent of our business comes from across the border in Rhode Island. Who would have thought?

It gets better. Now that we've proven Davio's can work in the suburbs, all kinds of new opportunities have opened up. People around the country have called, asking us to open in their suburban developments. I have turned some of these offers down, but others I have accepted. Simon Malls, the world's largest mall operator, called and asked us to re-create a Davio's in their mall in Atlanta's Buckhead section; it was a great opportunity to expand our brand into a new region, so I said yes. When Shari Redstone of National Amusements approached me to open up a Davio's at a new development in the wealthy Boston suburb of Chestnut Hill, I also agreed. We were also persuaded to open in a lifestyle center in my hometown of Lynnfield, Massachusetts. As I write this, I don't know for sure that these efforts at expansion will work out, but I have a good feeling. One thing is certain: I never would have had these opportunities if I hadn't been willing to listen to Jonathan and evolve our core concept. Ten years from now, we might have more suburban Davio's than urban locations.

This leads to a second point. If you do it right, expanding your operations can be a powerful way to *change* your operations so that they all stay fresh. We used our expansion to Philly as a way to test a concept that we ultimately rolled out in our core market, Boston. Once we opened in Boston, we took the great new chairs and upholstery we designed for that location and wound up installing them in Philly, too, followed by Boston's larger menu and great new bathroom design. Nowadays, anytime we open a new location, we try out new things that, if successful, we transfer back to our existing locations. We spent much of 2012 and 2013 planning for the grand opening of a Davio's in midtown Manhattan. The concept is similar to our other Davio's Northern Italian Steakhouses, but smaller, more refined, and more upscale. In creating the new menu, we found and tested that new machine from Italy I mentioned earlier that makes amazing fresh pasta. The thing works so well that we're now purchasing it for our other restaurants, too.

A third point, which follows in turn, is to pursue gradual change. Yes, sometimes you have to make a bold step, like we did when we let go of our Newbury Street location. But to extend the shelf life of your existing concept, it's important to make incremental improvements all along. As the owner you're the "keep it fresh" guy—all day, every day—and you need to inspire the rest of your team to do that, too. I'm constantly looking around for things to improve in every restaurant. By temperament I'm the kind of person who gets bored pretty quickly; I like to try things out and change things up. When I worked for UniFirst, I saw that they were constantly altering or updating parts of their operations as they expanded. First they redid their delivery trucks; next thing I knew, I was walking into the plant and finding out that they had new machines. They were always investing in their properties, always trying to get better and innovate. That made a big impression on me.

These days, I have our restaurants upgrade our physical plant *before* problems get too bad. Why? Because it's a lot easier and cheaper to fix a small problem than to fix a big one. If you're starting up a new restaurant, I would advise that you budget 2 percent of your sales every year for reinvestment into your physical plant. This means for every $1 million in annual sales that you do, you should set aside up to $20,000 to put back into upgrading your place.

But that's just the beginning. In terms of our internal processes, I tell our sales force to bring me new ideas every week or two—a new promotion to hold, a new set of people to approach for business. We just rolled out a new incentive for salespeople, sending them on a swanky vacation to Puerto Rico if they hit a certain sales target. My father had done things like that at UniFirst. "It's better to give someone memories than cash," he used to tell me. "They'll never remember who gave them the cash, but they'll always remember who sent them on a fantastic trip." Our chefs are constantly on the Internet checking out other restaurants and menus, or buying new cookbooks and food magazines. I think a menu is a great barometer of how fresh a restaurant is staying. Let's say you've been open ten years. Look at your menu when you first opened, and look at it today. If it's exactly the same, then chances are you're in trouble. I would hope that at least three quarters of your menu today is different from when you first started.

But probably no more than three quarters. My fourth point: As much as you need to evolve, you also need to maintain core elements—be it on the menu, or in your decor, or in other key aspects of your operation—that define your brand. When we reopened on Arlington Street, we kept our classic dishes, such as Penne Smoked Chicken and our Bolognese sauce. The chef Gordon Hamersley, a friend of mine, has had a special roast chicken dish on his menu since 1987. I swear to God, it's the best roast chicken you've ever had in your life! He's changed his menu a thousand times over the past twenty-five years, but that dish is still on it. Some people just like eating the same food every time they come to you, so you have to give them that. But most of the menu will and should change over time. A similar point holds true for all companies. Change your "menu" of offerings, but be sure to keep those mainstay offerings that you're known for and that people come back for time and again. Like our Pasta Bolognese (see next page).

~

When I was in college, my roommate Mark and I would drive up to Maine almost every winter weekend to ski at Sugarloaf. On the way we used to stop at Jimmy's, a gas station and diner on Route 4 in Auburn, Maine. One October day, we played a game of backgammon, with the winner getting dinner at Jimmy's. I lost, which meant that I would need to spend $10 or $15 picking up the tab for Mark the next time we had a ski weekend.

Pasta Bolognese

Cook ¼ **pound prosciutto,** diced, in a large pot until crispy. Add **1 finely chopped garlic clove, 1 large diced white onion, 1 diced carrot**, and **1 or 2 diced celery stalks,** and cook for 4 minutes. Then add **1 pound ground beef, 1 pound ground pork,** and **1 pound ground veal** and cook thoroughly, making sure it's all well mixed. Add **1 bay leaf** and cook ingredients together for 15 minutes, stirring frequently. Next, add in **2 (32-ounce) cans whole San Marzano tomatoes** that you've crushed by hand and reduce heat to low, bringing the mixture to a simmer. Leave it like this for 2 hours, stirring occasionally. Prepare **1 to 1½ pounds pasta** according to package directions (we love tagliatelle or rigatoni for this dish). Add **2 ounces pasta water** to the Bolognese sauce as well as **2 tablespoons butter.** Mix a small amount of the Bolognese sauce into the cooked pasta, then top with the remaining sauce. Serve right away!

A few months later, it was time for Mark to collect. We headed up to Sugarloaf and were shocked to turn the corner on Route 4 and see that Jimmy's was no longer there. In place of the gas station and diner, Jimmy had built a huge new building in which there now was a fancy restaurant. What a huge, huge difference! The servers wore tuxedos, and the check came to $100 rather than the usual $10 or $15. It was ridiculous, given the location—and I was pretty bummed that I would have to buy Mark dinner there instead of at the old Jimmy's.

Unfortunately, the new Jimmy's didn't even make it until the end of the ski season. By March it had closed, never to reopen. Jimmy had lost everything. He had gone *way* too far in his drive to stay fresh, getting away from the core of what he did well. Maybe a fancy restaurant was always his dream, but he should have expanded his gas station/diner model rather than going so far upscale. It stands today as a cautionary tale, and it was in the back of my mind when I first opened Arlington Street.

A fifth piece of advice: As you expand and freshen up your business, don't overload yourself. I pulled off our expansions in Philadelphia, Patriot Place, Atlanta, and elsewhere by delegating to others, especially the chefs and general managers I hired for each location. I mentioned Ettore in Philadelphia—he was critical to helping me get that location off the ground. In 2013, I opened up three locations at the same time, which wouldn't have been possible if I hadn't had a team of people on the ground I could count on. In fact, one of the great pleasures I take in expanding is the opportunity to promote long-time team members to new positions of responsibility in the company. If the company is growing and improving its operations to be more competitive, our people can grow with us.

This leads me to a sixth and final point. Don't make the mistake that some restaurateurs make and grow *because* you want to find places for your up-and-coming team members. If you expand, do it for the right reasons. I'll talk about my mistakes and failures in another chapter, but one mistake I made in Providence was opening that location because I wanted to keep my talented chefs and assistant managers. I knew they were gunning for promotions, and I needed places for them to grow. Many restaurateurs do what I did and expand to keep key people happy. Big mistake! Sometimes, you do have to let your good people leave. You can't think primarily about keeping them. Instead, you have to consider what is best for the brand and for your business. Embrace change and expand to keep your entire business fresh, but don't force it. Look for more natural or organic opportunities to evolve your business.

I lied. The sixth point above isn't the final lesson about staying fresh. There is one more: As your business grows and evolves, you have to be ready and willing not merely to welcome in the new, but say good-bye to the old. I've recounted how we moved our Newbury Street location, but that's not all we did when we opened up on Arlington Street. We also wound up not renewing the lease on our location just across the river in Cambridge. This restaurant was similar to the original Davio's—same menu, same smaller format, and exquisite cuisine thanks to our longtime chef Paul King. It was also quite profitable. Unfortunately, our clientele who had come to like the new Davio's would sometimes go to Cambridge and find a very different dining experience. It was hurting our brand. I would get e-mails that said, "Steve, the food at Cambridge is great, but you have to do something about the decor at that place; it's nothing like Arlington."

Our lease at Cambridge was up, and seeing how well we were doing on Arlington, our landlords wanted to increase our rent. It didn't make sense for us to pump a lot of money into renovations, and in any case, physical space constraints would have made it impossible to re-create fully the Arlington dining experience there. It was a tough decision, but I made it. Great things lay before us as a company; Cambridge, unfortunately, was our past.

Every business needs a good kick in the rear—both little kicks and big ones. For someone like me, that's a good thing. If you enjoy the challenge of business as much as I do, if you love imagining what could be, if you're committed to constantly doing better today than you did yesterday, then you're in for a wild, exciting ride. Davio's today is primarily an East Coast, urban brand. When I look to the future, I see us as a nation-wide brand, in places like Washington, DC, Chicago, Vegas, and San Francisco. Our menu will continue to evolve, as will the look and feel of our restaurants. We'll change the colors, the chairs, the rugs, the silverware. I can't predict where food trends will go five or ten years from now, but I do know I'll be watching them carefully and looking for opportunities to serve our guests even better than we do now.

When I think about keeping it fresh, I always think about my dad. He may be well into his eighties, but guess what? He's got a computer, and it has kept him going. I got him one for his eightieth birthday. While he was working, his assistant June Gallo took care of most of his communication. Now a whole new slice of life has opened up to him. He's constantly checking the Internet—and e-mailing me, although mostly to ask about bringing him meatballs. We can't just let life happen to us and hope we'll stay vibrant as we age. We have to commit ourselves to staying young, staying fresh. Everything dies—people as well as companies. But we can prolong the time we have. If you're starting or running your own company, I hope you'll follow my dad's example. I know I have, and both life and business keep on getting better.

Restaurant Lessons to Live By

Sometimes you have to take what you build and blow . . . it . . . up!

Don't take crazy risks. Think creatively about your business all along, and when it comes time to make a big move, you'll know what to do.

Keeping it fresh doesn't mean being totally original. Look for your own Grill 23 as inspiration to tweak what you're doing.

Be bold. If you're a city boy, maybe the suburbs aren't as scary as you think.

Keeping it fresh isn't a one-time thing. It's an all-the-time thing. Do it incrementally, little by little. Budget for it. And have fun with it.

CHAPTER ELEVEN

Restaurants Are Only the Beginning

There's another way to keep your business healthy over the long term besides refreshing your core product or concept: Branch out into a whole new realm!

As successful as Davio's has been, I've worked hard to diversify, not merely into different geographic areas, but beyond our core business. Once I bought Davio's, we pretty quickly began catering weddings, bar mitzvahs, and engagement parties in response to requests from guests. *Wow,* I thought, *this is great! It's like having a second restaurant.* Years later, when I opened at the Royal Sonesta Hotel in Cambridge, we began to handle a lot of private functions. Guests holding their weddings in the ballroom (and working with Royal Sonesta's catering operation) would have their rehearsal dinners with us. This business was so lucrative that we eventually hired Donna Wolfe in Cambridge as our first sales manager dedicated solely to booking and overseeing private functions. Our new Arlington Street location had almost half its seating capacity dedicated to private functions, and today I wouldn't open a restaurant without budgeting space for that use.

I participate in a number of other businesses as well. I am in packaged foods, run a take-out counter, and have helped start an online restaurant reservation company. I'm even writing and selling a book! I am always looking for the next business venture—and not merely because I'm looking for profits. From a risk standpoint it's smart to have your hand in many different things. That way, if one business tanks, you still have the others. Stuff happens, and it's best to cover yourself. In 2013, a huge snowstorm brought business in our New England restaurants to a standstill for days and cost us tens of thousands of dollars in lost sales. We had no problem with our cash flow, though; a $50,000 check from our packaged food venture happened to arrive at the same time. It was a small illustration of the blessings of diversification.

Over the long term the main thing that diversification can offer is name recognition that extends and strengthens your brand. Celebrity chefs like Wolfgang Puck, Emeril Lagasse, and Mario Batali all sell food in the world beyond their restaurants. As a result, they have become known to a wider audience, and more and more business opportunities of all kinds open up to them. Their core businesses—their restaurants—only become stronger. As I've become more established, I've asked myself why I can't do the same thing. True, I'm not a national television celebrity like they are, but can't I still expand the reach of Davio's and take my business to the next level? That's how you *get* to be a national television celebrity. It's also how you ensure that your brand survives. You grow it.

If you're just starting out, in restaurants or any business, be aggressive about branching out. Don't think that brand extensions are just for the big guys. As soon as you're able, enter a new business. Do what you know best: If you're good as a handyman, fix up condos. If you've always understood money, invest in mutual funds. Easiest and best of all, start with a business adjacent to your core operation. A restaurateur doesn't need a lot of capital to bottle her special recipe barbecue sauce or the salad dressing her in-house guests love. If you don't have a wide distribution network, start by selling it at farmers' markets or in local stores. Every little bit of brand exposure helps. And before you know it, more people will know who you are, your core business will thrive, and small opportunities will lead to bigger opportunities. Wolfgang Puck, watch out!

Sometimes, brand extensions take on exciting lives of their own. That's what happened with my packaged food business. It started off in 2007 as one of the crazier efforts I've made to keep our restaurants fresh. Five years later, it's a $10 million business and growing rapidly. We're in three thousand stores in forty states, including Costco, BJs, and Stop & Shop. I've even become a partner in the factory that produces them. And we're continuing to create and roll out new food products.

This is how it all began. One Monday in 2002, I was eating our family meal (what we call our staff meals) at our Davio's in Philadelphia. The food was good—it always is—but I noticed something strange. Someone had set out a plate of spring rolls, and they were delicious!

I asked Chef Dave Boyle where the spring rolls came from. Had he raided a Chinese place down the block?

"Well, you know, my wife's from Vietnam. She was making spring rolls this week and I had some cheese steak mix, so I put it in one of her wrappers."

They were out of this world. Crispy. Cheesy. Rich, meaty flavor. I couldn't stop eating them! I snagged three more for my plate. I got an idea. "Hey, Dave, we should put these on the menu!"

Dave laughed. "Yeah, right."

"I'm serious." I bit into another. "These are just incredible. Our guests would love them."

Dave looked at me like I was crazy. "How can a Northern Italian steakhouse sell spring rolls?"

I totally disagreed with him. I looked over at Ettore, our general manager. "Ettore, what do you think?"

Ettore looked up from his plate. "I don't know, Steve. Let's give it a shot. Who knows what'll happen."

Normally I don't push things on the chefs (I usually try to reason with them and get them to all agree), but these spring roll things were blowing my mind. I just had to get them on the bar menu. Good thing: People loved them! Word got out, and guests began coming in specifically for the spring rolls. Other restaurants started copying us and creating their own versions. Pretty cool, I thought. *Philadelphia* magazine gave them a Best of Philly award, which brought even more people in. Soon spring rolls were on our permanent menus, and we've never taken them off.

As great as the spring rolls were, I didn't immediately think to introduce them in our Boston-area restaurants. I figured this was a local thing—a cheese steak item in Philadelphia, the city that invented cheese steak.

A couple of years later, Eric Swartz and Steve Brown, our head chefs at Arlington Street, and I were reworking some menu items, trying to freshen things up. I thought of the spring rolls. "Hey guys," I said, "you know those spring rolls we do in Philadelphia? What do you think about putting them on our bar menu here?"

"Huh?" Steve said, staring at me.

"I'm serious," I said.

Steve and Eric both shook their heads. "That's a Philly thing."

I thought about it for a moment. Philly cheese steak spring rolls were a specific thing that Philly did, and these guys just weren't into it. "You know what? Let's just do it. I've got a good feeling here."

We put them on the bar menu, and once again, they flew out the kitchen door. Up and down our bar, people were sitting in front of plates of Philly cheese steak spring rolls, having the time of their lives. Despite the rolls' popularity, I didn't think that anything more would come of them. Then one night in 2006, Jonathan Kraft came in to Arlington Street for dinner. He was at Table 60 over in the corner, entertaining a couple friends from Harvard Business School. He called me over. "Steve, I've got to tell you, these Philly roll things, where did this idea come from?"

I told him the story.

He pointed to his half-eaten plate of rolls. "Well, I think you need to do something with them."

"Like what?"

"Sell them to more people. Other restaurants. Caterers. Hotels. Stores."

I laughed. "Jonathan, how am I going to do that? I'm a restaurant guy. I wouldn't know the first thing about that."

"Well, you need to look into it."

His friends nodded their heads. "I totally agree," one of them said.

I walked away thinking that Jonathan had a marble loose or something. Me, selling spring rolls in stores? How would I do that? And who would buy them?

⌁

Jonathan's idea stuck with me. Again and again over the next few months, I found myself fantasizing about it. Could I? Should I? Jonathan was no dummy. I've said it before: He is the smartest person I've ever met—and I've met Rhodes Scholars. He seemed pretty serious about the rolls. Maybe there was something to this.

I started to research how I could produce a packaged food product. I couldn't just make the rolls in our kitchen; there were government regulations I had to satisfy for mass production to make sure nobody got sick. Regulations aside, I was really worried about screwing up the product somehow and hurting our brand. I couldn't risk that. If we were going ahead with this project, we had to do it right.

Fortunately, I then met Stephanie Hernan, owner of Yankee Trader Seafood, an established packaged food company with a production plant a half-hour drive from Boston. "We can make your product," she said. We fine-tuned the recipe, created a package, and went into production. She received USDA approval to handle meat and to make our rolls (previously she had been approved only for seafood). In early 2008, when the product was finally ready for sale, I called up Jonathan Kraft. "Hey, Jonathan, remember how you told me I should sell my spring rolls on a bigger scale? Well, I got it done and am ready to find some buyers."

"Bring them by the stadium," he said. "I'd like to try them out."

I dropped by with a box of our rolls. He and his dad Robert tried them. "These are great!" Jonathan said. "Just as good as in the restaurant. We'd like to serve them at the stadium. One thing, though: You have to get Brad [the stadium's corporate chef] to taste it. See what he thinks."

Jonathan may have been the boss, but he wasn't about to ram my product down his chef's throat. So I went to see Brad and cook up a batch for him. Prior to working at Gillette Stadium, Brad had worked for Hyatt for years and was a pretty savvy guy. He took a bite and his eyes lit up. "Oh my God, these are so fucking good!"

I couldn't tell if he really thought they were good, or if he was just humoring me. When I asked him, he responded through a mouthful, "Steve, you have no idea how happy I am with these. You're Jonathan's buddy, so I knew I'd have to take them, but I'm so happy that they are this good."

That was our first account—Gillette Stadium. They were an instant hit; we sold out our shipment of 1,000 rolls during the first game. Brad became a huge advocate for us. When you tell buyers in the food industry that you're being sold in Gillette Stadium, and you have a well-known guy like Brad singing your praises, you can make headway. I approached food distributors who sold to Davio's and asked them to try our rolls. The big distributor Agar saw how successful we were at Gillette Stadium and agreed to have its own salespeople push the rolls to restaurants, caterers, hotels, and others that they served. The same thing happened with Sysco Philadelphia. In some cases the buyer decided to resell our rolls to end consumers as a Davio's branded product; in other cases they didn't.

By 2009 we decided we were ready for retail. Stephanie's Yankee Trader seafood products were already in a lot of stores, such as Stop & Shop, Roche Bros., and Big Y, so she was able to get appointments for us with frozen food buyers. We got a few sales initially, but many more the following year when we redesigned our package. Today, retail sales are about 50 percent of our total packaged foods business. We have seven different flavors, including chicken parm, shrimp cojita, buffalo chicken, macaroni and cheese, rueben, and salmon. I initially had a licensing agreement with Yankee Trader, giving me a share of sales, but sales of the spring rolls grew so quickly that I was soon accounting for half of that company's sales. Feeling that I was leaving money on the table, I renegotiated a deal that gave me 40 percent of Yankee Trader. In addition to spring rolls, I am now invested in everything the company sells, including products like fish cakes, crab cakes, scallops and shrimp wrapped in bacon, and calamari. Davio's branded products currently account for 60 percent of Yankee Trader's sales. Responding to requests from our guests, we're continually trying out new product ideas. Watch for them at a store near you!

Now, perhaps you're wondering: What's an Italian-Portuguese guy like me doing selling Philly cheese steak spring rolls at places like BJs when my core business is an upscale Northern Italian steakhouse? How can a spring roll business possibly be good for the Davio's brand? Am I confusing my brand identity, or taking it too far downscale?

I would argue that the packaged food business is working wonders for the Davio's brand. Consumers see the Davio's brand name when they do their grocery shopping, and if they purchase our products, they see it every time they open their freezer as well as my face, right there on the package! It's a powerful thing, especially since they're associating our brand with a quality product that they enjoy. You can't buy that kind of brand awareness with your typical advertising or marketing budget alone. (Of course, I also have friends who are freaked out to see me every time they open the freezer. But, they assure me, they've learned to position the box a certain way so my picture is blocked. I do the same thing at my house.) People I meet ask me about the spring rolls all the time, and many guests try out our restaurants after first trying and liking our frozen spring rolls. They come in and ask, "Hey, is the guy on the box here?" In some cases guests actually ask me to autograph the box for them.

But I did worry at first. I understand how important it is to be clear about your brand—what it means and what it does. I decided to move ahead with the spring rolls because I felt that our core brand was already well entrenched in people's minds. Yes, I think all companies should from the outset look into diversification, but start-ups should take care to choose projects that keep closely to their brand and don't contradict it. It would have been difficult to have taken a new brand and done what we've done with spring rolls, but Davio's restaurant has been around for almost three decades. People in our markets know us, and they know what we do. The Davio's brand tends to *enhance* the stature of the packaged food products, rather than the packaged food products diminishing the Davio's brand. Keep in mind, we're selling the exact same handmade products we use in our fine-dining establishments. These products are restaurant quality, which gives them a premium feel on store shelves.

If you're trying a brand extension, never put out a cheap product just to make a quick buck. The brand has to remain paramount. And if your brand is well enough established to handle a given extension, make sure you still proceed thoughtfully and strategically. When I open a restaurant in a new market, I do not feature spring rolls on the dinner menu. I might put them on the bar menu, since you can generally be a bit freer there without people noticing. But I keep the main menu clearly aligned with our overall concept so that the local market gets a chance to know and understand what Davio's is. After a period of time, we can start to stretch and mold the brand a little by promoting our brand extensions. I should add that although spring rolls aren't on the menu in a new market, people usually ask for them anyway. We serve them, and they wind up becoming a kind of hidden secret, which is fun for guests and for us, too.

There's so much you can do to extend an established brand. Even before we came out with the spring rolls, we were already pushing in new directions by unveiling the Davio's take-out counter adjacent to our Arlington Street location. You'll remember that when our landlord came up with the idea, I was initially skeptical. But I wound up taking a risk. As I mentioned earlier, the counter now brings in close to $1 million in incremental revenue without cannibalizing our existing restaurant sales. The guest who wants a $6 sandwich is not about to eat lunch at our restaurant. Meanwhile, nobody ever used to call us to create deli platters or pizzas for an office luncheon, but they do now. We open in the morning for breakfast, and by 2:00 p.m. each day, everything at the counter is gone.

As both the packaged food and take-away counter examples suggest, one way to find opportunities for diversification is simply to pay attention and wait for exciting ideas to present themselves. But you can also find them by noticing problems that arise in your industry and seeing if you can start a business that solves them.

Many restaurants around the country today use a system called OpenTable. Through it guests can book reservations online, and restaurants can manage those reservations and overall guest traffic using on-site computer equipment that OpenTable provides. It's a brilliant solution and a great improvement to the manual, pen-and-paper method that we used back in the '80s to record and keep track of reservations. The problem is it's too expensive! OpenTable charges $1 per person for guests that book through its website—that's $6 right off the check for a table of six. OpenTable also charges you $0.25 per person if the guest books through your own website, and it charges for the computer equipment—a total of $2,000 or more a month for some restaurants. To make it even worse, if a guest makes a reservation on OpenTable, the company e-mails a couple of days later to recommend other, similar restaurants nearby. That means it's sending my guests to my competition—and charging me for the privilege! OpenTable might make sense for urban restaurants, since many diners need a service to help them identify and narrow down their restaurant options. In suburban areas like Foxboro and Lynnfield, however, guests rarely use OpenTable to book with us. We're paying a lot for very little benefit.

Remember my friend Jeff Gates, the server who cleaned a mysterious substance off the seat at our infamous Table 7? He has since gone on to open up several restaurants of his own. One day in 2011, he called to tell me how fed up he was with OpenTable. I told him I was fed up, too—that the whole situation reminded me of how American Express exploited restaurateurs back in the day. Here, again, we seemed to have a company that was thinking more about its own needs than the restaurateur's needs. Jeff told me that he and a friend of his, Van Garrett, were working on a project called UReserv, which would be an alternative to OpenTable. The company would be just as good as OpenTable and only charge restaurants a monthly $30 fee, taking advantage of low overhead and making most of its money through advertising on the UReserv site. Would I be willing to help them out financially? And would I have any ideas on how they could build the business?

The answer was yes . . . and yes! I wound up purchasing a piece of the company. The investment was small enough that it wouldn't hobble me financially, and it gave me an opportunity to help other restaurateurs and the industry as a whole. If all went well, I'd make some money and further diversify my business.

My idea about how to build the business involved approaching a marketing company called Rewards Network, which connects some ten thousand restaurants with airlines, giving guests airline miles when they use their credit cards for dining purchases. If we could get Rewards Network's large sales force to sell UReserv to their restaurant guests around the country, we would do incredibly well. Since Davio's is a participating Rewards Network merchant and I know the CEO and other top executives, Jeff, Van, and I flew to Chicago to make the pitch. Our local Rewards Network rep, Gina, also helped out a lot in setting up this meeting. The executives loved the system and did a deal with us. We already had gotten three hundred restaurants to contract with UReserv, and as of this writing we will likely have thousands more joining up. We're already phasing out OpenTable at Davio's, and in our new locations, we will work only with UReserv.

As my experience with UReserv suggests, it pays to keep an open mind. Opportunities are everywhere—if you're ready to seize them, and if you can partner with people capable of handling parts of the business unfamiliar to you. In the case of both UReserv and packaged foods, the strong, quality partnerships we've forged with industry professionals have allowed us to participate. Jeff's friend Van (who is now my friend, too) runs UReserv, and I mainly take the role of a silent investor. I wouldn't have had time for it if I had had to do all the legwork myself. As far as our packaged food goes, I didn't have to exhaustively engineer a production process or take years developing sales leads in retail stores. Stephanie and Yankee Trader did all that. All I had to do, besides working with our corporate chef Rodney to develop new products, was assist with sales. I've accompanied Stephanie all over the country— to San Francisco, LA, Seattle, San Diego, Houston, Chicago, DC, Atlanta. Each time, I was in and out in a day, showing guests our products. It wasn't heavy lifting. I've been able to focus on what I do best, building and running restaurants.

I also felt comfortable becoming more involved in both endeavors because of the talented people I've got helping me run my own restaurants—Ettore as director of operations, Rodney as corporate chef, and the general managers at each location. Thanks to their support, I can go to the Yankee Trader factory for a couple hours in the morning and come to a Davio's in the early afternoon, without worrying that our core business is suffering. Every day, I make sure that I do Davio's stuff. I am a restaurateur to the bone and always will be. At the same time, because of my team, I am not forced to give it 100 percent of my time.

With a strong team in place, you can do almost anything. In the absence of a strong team, I would think twice about diversifying too far, since you might only wind up overwhelmed and unhappy. Build your brand, and prove to yourself over time that you can sustain it and keep it fresh. As you become more and more confident and stable, branch out into more and more things. That's what I did, and the rewards have been great. Something tells me that the best is yet to come.

~~

Not everybody can start a packaged food business and wind up in three thousand stores almost overnight. I have been incredibly lucky. But as I said earlier, even if you don't have a lot of extra time and money, even if running your core business seems like a handful, try just dipping your toe into another business. Start small; stick with something you already know. If you've got a landscaping business, try growing and selling flowers or heirloom tomatoes. If you run a dance studio, try marketing a line of dance clothing on the web. Whatever you do, push yourself a little, so that you don't become too comfortable. Expanding your brand outward—in addition to keeping it fresh at its core—will help you keep your business strong, vibrant, and relevant. It's a great way to renew the old enthusiasm and entrepreneurial spirit you channeled when you first started your brand.

Thirty years into it, I'm not nearly done expanding and extending the Davio's brand. As I write this, we're in the process of unveiling a line of high-quality, reasonably priced Davio's branded wine, which we'll sell in-house and in liquor stores close to our restaurants. In the years to come, I want to see us everywhere. Davio's olive oil. Davio's restaurant-quality cooking pans. Davio's cookbooks. Davio's San Manzano tomatoes, home grown on our own farm. Additional Davio's specialty food items, such as Italian entrées in the frozen food section. As long as it's related to what I know about—preparing, selling, and serving food—I'm interested.

Davio's Tomato Soup
(in a Grocer's Aisle Near You Someday?)

Grab a stock pot—we're making some soup today! First, melt **3 ounces cubed, unsalted butter** over medium heat in that pot. Now add in **1 large white onion, sliced,** and cook until translucent. Add **2 (28-ounce) cans San Marzano tomatoes** that you've crushed by hand and **1 quart chicken stock.** Let this simmer for 1 hour. Come back and add in **1 loaf Italian bread, cubed.** Let that simmer for 45 minutes. Come back and remove the pot from heat and let it cool. After it's cooled off a bit, puree the mixture until it's nice and smooth. When you're ready to serve, bring the soup back to a simmer. Add in some **salt and pepper** to taste. Throw in **2 tablespoons each of julienned basil and chopped parsley.** I love to garnish my tomato soup with soft goat cheese and chive crostini.

Years from now, when Davio's is a national brand and we've got restaurants coast to coast, cookbooks in every store, and products and services on sale that I can't even imagine, I still won't retire. Restaurant guys don't give it all up for golf;

they don't wait around to die—it just doesn't happen! Even my father has advised me never to retire, since he feels he gave up his own career too early. So I'll diversify even further—into charity work. That's my endgame, and I've been inspired to pursue it by a Boston-area hero of mine, Don Rodman. This longtime car dealer, now in his eighties, has raised over $85 million to help at-risk kids. How wonderful it must be to wake up every morning and wonder, "How many people in the world can I help today?" How wonderful, too, to know you have the respect and admiration of the community that made your brand so successful. Following Don's example, and that of other successful people I know, I'll be excited to focus on what I've tried to do all along, and what has always given me pleasure—giving back.

You know what? Restaurants really are just the beginning. For us owners, for our teams, and for the community at large.

Restaurant Lessons to Live By

Don't just do one thing. You can't predict when a snow-storm will hit and that $50,000 check from your other business will come in handy.

Figure out who the smartest person you've ever met is. When they suggest a crazy new business idea to you, LISTEN!

An Italian-Portuguese guy selling Philly cheese steak rolls in a Northern Italian steakhouse? Hey, you never know.

Before you go nuts with brand extensions, make sure your core brand is rock solid, get some strong partners, and assemble a team in-house to back you up.

The next time you see a company taking advantage of people in your industry, like OpenTable does, don't get mad—get even. Start a new business and become their competitor.

Never stop diversifying. Restaurant guys never retire.

CHAPTER TWELVE

Bad Things Happen. Deal with It.

Many of my most pivotal, life-changing insights arrived unexpectedly, in a flash. One of them, as childish as it may sound, came during the last football game of my senior year at Lynnfield High School. I was the captain and we were playing our biggest rivals, North Reading, on Thanksgiving Day—a game Lynnfield hadn't lost in fifteen years. My older brother, whose shoes I was trying to fill, had never lost a game to North Reading. The whole town was there, all my friends, former players—everyone I knew.

Our team took the field, and from the first snap, things didn't go well. We couldn't get a rhythm going. Two of our star players got knocked out with injuries. By halftime we were down 27–0. It was *so* embarrassing—a total disaster.

During halftime I was in the locker room, resting. None of the other guys were around. Coach Rodan came over and sat down next to me. "Look, Steve. Let's just make sure the team doesn't quit. Who cares what the score is? Let's show North Reading what Lynnfield is made of. Nobody quits. *Never* quit."

This was my Knute Rockne moment. Coach Rodan had been my and my sister's history teacher and had coached my brother. He came to one of my Pop Warner games when I was in eighth grade and gave me words of encouragement. He was like God to me. His words hit home. I gathered the team around and gave them the same talk. "Who cares what the score is?" I said. "Let's go out there and do the best we can."

We fought to the very end. We didn't win. It was still a massacre: 30–0. One of the worst days of my life. But at least we didn't quit.

A couple of weeks later, Coach Rodan came up to me to talk about the turkey trophy that the winning team traditionally received. "What are you doing this afternoon? We've had the trophy for fifteen years. Can you take it over to North Reading? Since you're the captain of the team, I think you should take it back."

I wasn't busy, so I took the trophy over to our rival school. The athletic director saw me come in. "Hey DiFillippo, I see there's our trophy."

I held it out for him to take. "Yeah, here you go."

He nodded down the hall. "Can you just take it over to the gym for me?"

"Sure."

He led me down the hall, and the next thing I knew I was walking with the trophy into the gymnasium, where the entire school had been assembled. The crowd was shouting, "Thirty to nothing! Thirty to nothing!"

The athletic director saw my shock. "Coach Rodan didn't tell you?"

"No, he didn't."

"Okay. You can go now."

I cried the whole way home. I was so embarrassed, not to mention annoyed at the coach for setting me up. When I got over those feelings, I found myself taking to heart Coach Rodan's basic message. *You never quit.* You just don't. I still believe that, most of the time. When things have gotten bad in our restaurants, I've kept going. I know I have to show up the next day, and the day after that, thinking of new things, trying to fix whatever problems I'm dealing with. A lot of people in business, and certainly in restaurants, are too quick to quit, and I'm here to say that you need to stay the course when the going gets tough.

Over time, though, I've come to realize that Coach Rodan wasn't quite telling me the whole truth about life. The whole truth is that you also have to know when to quit, and when that time comes, you have to be brutal about pulling the plug. Here, too, restaurant guys come up short. We're the ultimate deniers. We don't like to admit that mistakes happen, that things didn't go our way—that we failed. We tend to pretend everything with the business is fine. Confronted by bad sales figures, most of us say, "We don't have a serious problem. We'll make a little change here or there. Hell, we'll redo the entire concept if we have to." In some cases, like the Black Cow restaurant described in chapter ten, that might work. But what if your location isn't good? Then no amount of redoing the concept will change a damn thing.

You can tell pretty quickly if a restaurant will make it. If that isn't happening, you're better off cutting your losses. You're probably not going to see a magical rebound once business is down. There are always exceptions, but generally, guests won't come back. Yet many owners struggle along and borrow money to stay in business. In the worst cases they max out their credit cards or even wind up bankrupt. It's all so unnecessary. If you want a way to lose a lot of money really fast and feel bad about it, then keep denying. But if you want to succeed over the long term, then you better swallow your pride, acknowledge that you've screwed up, put the pieces back together, and find a way to move on to bigger and better things. There is no other way.

How do you know when it's quitting time? *You know.* That little voice in your head starts speaking up, and it's harder and harder to ignore it. Sales dry up. People stop coming in. Bad reviews pop up a little too frequently on Yelp (man, do I hate that thing). Servers complain and start to leave because they aren't making any money. You can't pay your vendors on time, and they start providing you with goods on a cash-only basis. You can't pay your meals taxes. I can always tell a restaurant is having financial trouble when I open up my local business journal and see it on the list of establishments that aren't paying meals taxes.

Sometimes, you still have a lot of guests coming in but they aren't spending enough, and you just can't turn a decent profit. You'll recall that this is what happened at our Brookline location, my first real failure in business. We opened the place in 1988, before the 1991 recession. We had an expensive building and had sunk a lot of money into renovations, but because we hadn't priced the menu properly, we couldn't make a good return. People in that suburban location weren't

Homemade Potato Gnocchi
(My Answer for When Times Get Tough)

This recipe makes 125 gnocchi, so make sure to invite some friends over. Boil **2¼ pounds russet potatoes** until tender. Drain the water, and then while the potatoes are still hot, peel and put them through a ricer. Set aside, and let them cool through and through. (Little tip: This can be done the day before.) On a large board form a "mountain" with the cooled and riced potatoes. Add **1½ cups sifted flour, ½ cup grated Parmigiano cheese,** and **¼ teaspoon each salt and pepper.** Make a hole at the top of the mountain and add **2 medium eggs** into the hole. Working by hand from the eggs out, begin mixing eggs with the potato and other ingredients until well blended. Cover the mixture with a slightly damp cloth or a bowl and let it rest for 30 minutes.

Come back and roll the dough by hand into eight 2-foot-long rolls, about the size of a quarter in diameter. Then cut each roll into ½-inch pieces. Delicately dust the pieces with flour and place them in a plastic container. Make sure there's only one layer per container and each piece has plenty of breathing room! Cover and freeze until ready to cook. (Another tip: Once the gnocchi are frozen, they can be transferred into ziplock bags so you don't have a bunch of plastic containers all piled up in your freezer. Oh, and gnocchi can be kept frozen up to 1 month.)

When you're ready to cook, take some gnocchi out of the freezer and bring 12 quarts salted water to a rapid boil. Add your gnocchi and then cover and cook until the water returns to a boil. I'd try using more than one pot when cooking, and I also advise that you cook only a handful of gnocchi at a time. If you jam too many together, you wind up with a watery potato soup! Now uncover the gnocchi and cook for an additional 2 minutes or until the gnocchi begins to float. Strain, add your favorite sauce, and serve immediately in a warm bowl.

Another technique you can try is to precook your gnocchi and then refreeze them. On the night you wish to serve them, you'll only need a few minutes to heat them up. Just throw them in the sauce, and you can spend more time drinking wine with your guests.

willing to spend as much for a meal as they were in down-town Boston, so our check averages were half of what I was expecting. And then the recession came along and sliced our revenues back even farther.

In retrospect, I should have cut my losses before the reces-sion, when the pattern of small to no profits became obvious. But profits from the Newbury Street Davio's were rolling in, so I thought I could mess with the concept and make the Brook-line location work. I didn't want to admit that my efforts there had failed. I was in denial!

In 1993 I teamed up with local restaurateur Jae Chung, renovated the Brookline Davio's, and replaced it with an Asian-fusion concept called Pacifico. Danny Wisel, a Cor-don Bleu–trained chef and great friend of mine, became the head chef. He worked with me to design a new menu, which included sushi and other Asian items but kept some of the Italian specialties that Davio's guests loved. I sunk $100,000 into renovations. And what happened?

Well, first I had problems with our Asian cooks, who insisted on being paid in cash without withholding for taxes. When I refused, Jae and I had a falling out, and he left. I brought in some new kitchen staff and then discovered that our Japanese sushi chefs weren't speaking with our Chinese personnel, who weren't speaking to the Thai team members. Not good. What *was* good was the food. Actually, it was incred-ible! But we still weren't making any money. It was the same problem: Our food costs were too high, and given our rela-tively small space, we couldn't get enough volume to pay for our building. I wasn't about to lower our food quality, so cut-ting food costs was a nonstarter. In 1997 we finally got out when a woman showed up on my doorstep and offered to buy the building. The real estate market was back, so luckily I wound up paying off a lot of our debt from the renovations. But that doesn't change the fact that I should have gotten out much earlier than I did from what was essentially a losing business and location.

⌐⌐

Live and learn, right? Not exactly. Sometimes you have to rub your nose in it again and again before you get the message. In 2006 I opened a new restaurant up the block from my successful Arlington Street Davio's. Called Avila (my mom's maiden name), it was an upscale Mediterranean place with a mixture of Spanish, Italian, French, Greek, and Portuguese dishes. It seemed like a solid business decision at the time. The Boston scene lacked this concept, and as our private functions business at Davio's was going through the roof, I figured that Avila could handle our overflow.

For the first year and a half, Avila had decent sales. With our current corporate chef Rodney at the helm, our food was really great, and we got solid reviews. But a combination of factors, including the 2007–08 recession and the state ban on pharmaceutical educational dinners that I described earlier, caused the restaurant to underperform. Also, our Davio's clientele didn't transfer over. We did manage to get a newer base of guests to come in—younger, more women—but it wasn't enough to make Avila profitable.

In retrospect, we screwed up a bit from the start. When we were creating Avila, Chef Rodney, my pal Phil the coffee guy, and I traveled to Spain and Portugal to collect ideas. Our initial vision was a funky place with crazy colors, a painted floor, unusual furniture, and more moderate price points. Our landlord Tony Pangaro didn't like that look and feel; he wanted a more upscale restaurant. Since he was chipping in $1 million for renovations, and since my lease gave him the right to refuse our plans, I had no choice but to agree.

I made Avila fancier and more expensive, turning off a section of guests who otherwise might have tried us. The restaurant was also too big, saddling us with a high overhead. Finally, Tony wouldn't let me put up awnings and signs for the restaurant, even though they would have brought in more traffic. I have all the respect in the world for Tony, but even brilliant minds like his get it wrong sometimes. When you partner with landlords, make sure from the outset that they share your vision. If they don't, you could wind up with a very different—and less profitable—business than you planned.

The biggest mistake was all mine: not getting out when I had the chance. At the end of our fifth year, right when it was becoming clear that Avila wouldn't be as profitable as our other restaurants, a broker came in with a buyer for the business. I judged his final offer too low and declined. Once again, I wasn't ready to admit that I had failed. I didn't know when to quit. What I should have done was calculate how much money I would lose if I held on to Avila for another year, two years, three years. If I had factored in these probable losses, the low offer I had been given might have seemed much more attractive. I could have sunk another $100,000 or $200,000 into rebranding Avila, but I probably would have wound up selling it anyway in a year or two, so the investment wouldn't have made sense. Better to simply swallow my losses now and learn the lesson of when to quit once and for all. As it turned out, I sold Avila in 2013 under very similar terms as I had previously been offered. Not a bad ending, when everything was said and done.

I don't mean to suggest that I haven't learned from my mistakes. I've screwed up many times over the years, and as a result I think I've gotten better at what I do. A great learning experience was our failed Davio's in Providence, Rhode Island. When we opened there in 1996, in the Biltmore Hotel, I was really excited. Providence was where my parents had grown up. I had roots in the city, and initially, I also had a great partner at the Biltmore, the co-owner, Bill. We got along well, and he supported us. For the first couple of years, we made money. Then Bill got out of the Biltmore, leaving me with a partner who had never liked Davio's; he made little secret of the fact that he wanted a big national chain to occupy the space. At every turn he made our life more difficult.

It was already difficult enough. One of the biggest problems we faced was labor. The Biltmore is a union hotel. Some of our team members didn't see any difference between themselves and the hotel's kitchen staff. Why should they receive less? If we didn't voluntarily pay premium wages, these team members would unionize and we'd be forced to pay even higher, union wages. So our labor costs were elevated from the beginning, which cut into our margins substantially.

By the late '90s another problem had cropped up. Our original manager had left, and his replacement, whom I had brought down from Boston, was in over his head. When starting a restaurant, you *always* have to hire local people to run the place. They understand the market better. They know what guests care about. They know who the local celebrities are. They know who to call to bring in business and resolve problems, and who not to call. Not having a local general manager or chef was possibly our biggest mistake there— and something I never did again. In fact, our Atlanta location, which opened in 2010, has been so successful precisely because of the expertise of our manager Claude, former head of the dining room at the Ritz Carlton in Buckhead.

Our problems continued. Our chef turned out to be a psycho and a drug addict. The staff was becoming sleazy and dishonest. As we opened our Philadelphia location in 1999, I found that I was dreading going down to Providence to check in on operations. In 2003 the hotel management came to me and asked if we wanted to leave. I jumped at the chance to be bought out of the lease. Our Arlington and Philadelphia restaurants had catapulted us to a new level of success. I just didn't need the headaches of Providence any longer. In the seven years we had been open there, I hadn't made very much money. What I did gain was some valuable wisdom that I've put to good use ever since: Be careful opening an independent restaurant in a union-run hotel. Always hire local talent. And make sure you hire a chef who isn't crazy!

Looking back, I see that Providence gave me the chance to forge a valuable contact with restaurant broker Mike Feldott, and it was thanks to his contacts that I wound up opening in Philadelphia. Without Mike, that opportunity never would

Sautéed Calamari
(Davio's Version of a Providence Specialty)

Put **1 ounce extra virgin olive oil** (Monini preferred) in a sauté pan over high heat. Then add **12 ounces fresh calamari** (rings and tentacles) and cook for 2 minutes. Remove the calamari from the pan, and set it aside. Add **1 small garlic clove, chopped,** into the pan and cook until it's golden brown. Deglaze with **3 ounces white wine.** Next, add **3 ounces heavy cream** and **¼ ounce anchovy paste** to the pan and reduce the heat by half. Stir in **a pinch of red pepper flakes.** Add your beautiful calamari and cook this all together for about 3 minutes or until hot. Add **salt and pepper** to your heart's delight. I suggest you serve it over sliced and grilled bread.

have happened. I probably wouldn't have brought the Northern Italian steakhouse concept back to Arlington Street, and I wouldn't have the kind of success I enjoy today. This leads to an important point about mistakes, failures, and disappointments: They aren't what they seem. Quite often, they wind up being blessings in disguise, leading to unimaginable future successes.

In 1997 I had a major dispute with our Newbury Street landlord over an option I had to extend the lease for five more years. The option said the rent would be pegged at a fair market value, but of course, we disagreed on what that was. (Another hard-learned lesson: Never sign a lease with a "market rent" option. You're setting yourself up for a dispute with your landlord. Always go for a fixed-term, fixed-rent lease.) The landlord, an older Italian guy, wanted $80 a square foot or something insane like that. No amount of talking brought him down, and it didn't help that he had never taken me seriously and called me a "college kid." The guy just didn't like me. So I brought my father, another older Italian guy, in to negotiate with him. My dad is a seasoned pro; as an executive at UniFirst, he had negotiated tough union deals all over the country.

My dad went in to meet with my landlord. They talked for a couple of hours. Afterward, my dad came back to me in shock. "You know, Steve, this guy is the worst ever! He is just awful. It did not go well. You better start looking for a new restaurant, because in five years, when your option is up, you gotta go. There is just no way that guy will negotiate a new lease with you."

My father even tried to buy the building from the landlord, but he wouldn't sell. It seemed he wanted to see me fail. I went home that night thinking, *Oh man, what am I going to do?* We wound up going to mediation and hiring an appraiser to determine what my rent would be for those next five years. The figure came back a lot closer to what I wanted—$40 rather than $80. We had won big, but the fight had cost $50,000 in legal fees and made me a permanent enemy of the landlord. I was devastated. Newbury Street was our signature restaurant. Business was better than ever. How would I ever be able to replicate that success in a different location?

It ended up being a huge blessing in disguise. If the landlord had not fought me, I would have continued on with Newbury Street and probably never would have taken the plunge in Philadelphia and the opportunity to try out the Northern Italian steakhouse concept there. Without Philly already working, I certainly wouldn't have sunk more than $1 million into a much bigger place on Arlington Street, and in turn, I wouldn't today be at Gillette Stadium or in Atlanta, since both of those deals flowed from that new Boston location. I wouldn't have a take-out operation attached to Arlington bringing in $1 million a year. Everything would be different. My company would be a much smaller, more local operation.

I now thank that stubborn old Italian guy for being a total jerk. He gave my career as a restaurateur the kick it needed. It didn't feel so great at the time, but in the long term, it was a gift. The landlord wound up selling the Newbury Street building and going back to Italy. Every so often, my dad says to me, "I wonder how that bastard is doing."

Have I told you my Officer Suckley story yet? I can't write this book without it! When I was in eighth grade, I had a business cutting people's lawns. As I got more and more accounts, it became too hard to use the small push lawnmower I had. Mr. Argeros, who lived right around the corner, let me borrow his much nicer riding lawnmower. I used it for a couple of weeks until one day I had the good sense to stick my hand in where the sprocket wheel was—while the motor was running. Not wanting to walk around the rest of my life attached to a lawn mower, I pulled my hand out and cut myself in the process. There was blood everywhere. I ran home. "Mom, mom! I just cut myself." Taking one look at my bloody, grease-covered hand, this woman, who had never before uttered a swear word, said, "You fucking cut your finger off!"

She wrapped up my hand, and my sister, then a college freshman, started shouting that I needed to go to the hospital. We got in the car, me in back and my sister in the passenger seat. As my mom drove down Main Street in our town, going her usual twenty-five miles per hour, I felt nauseous. "Pull into the police station!" my sister shouted. "We're going too slow! We've got to get him to the hospital!"

We pulled into the police station—just as I was throwing up. Two officers ran out and put me in the back of a cruiser. One guy drove while the other, Officer Suckley, sat in back to comfort me. We did eighty miles an hour down Summer Street to get to Lynn Hospital, the closest one. The doctors took a look and then my mother arrived with strict orders. "Nobody touch him! I'm gonna get a plastic surgeon to look at it." I waited for two hours without any pain medication for the plastic surgeon to arrive. When he finally did, he gave me a shot of medication and clipped off the bone in my finger, which was sticking out at an odd angle.

I got used to life with only nine and a half fingers. Four years went by. I was now seventeen, a senior at Lynnfield High School and a member of the football team. We played Newburyport, who had been 38–0 and whom we had never beaten before, and wound up topping them 6–0. It was front-page news, a big deal in our town, and to celebrate, we had a party at our house. Back then, the drinking age was eighteen and having a few beers at home wasn't as taboo as it is now for high school students. I was only seventeen, but big deal—what's a few months? The DiFillippo house was known for its parties because we had a lot of space, including a big basement. Bands would come and play, and we had big crowds. My parents loved having all the kids over, and of course we kids loved it, too.

Our party that night lasted until about 1:00 a.m. My girl-friend at the time was supposed to have been home by midnight, and I had to drive her. We got in the car, and I cruised way too fast down Main Street. I saw police lights and pulled over to the side. Damn! I was hoping to get into Boston University, and I was a little tipsy since I had been drinking. Driving was a stupid thing to have been doing, to say the least. I was probably doing sixty in a thirty-mile-an-hour zone. And I was drinking underage.

As the officer came up to talk to me, I was really nervous. I rolled my window down and got my license out. And who do you think I saw? Officer Suckley! He took a look at my license. "Oh my God. Steve DiFillippo—is that you?" I expected that he would frown and give me a stern lecture about driving too fast or drinking. Instead he smiled. "Hey, let me see that finger!" I showed him my finger. "Wow, they did a great job! Hey, great game today!" He shot me a look of admiration. "So cool to beat Newburyport. I'm really proud of you guys. Boy, you had a big party at your house tonight. But you know, you better slow down."

I couldn't believe it. He was going to let me off. "I'm so sorry, officer. My girlfriend has to be home. That's why I'm driving fast."

"Well, do me a favor. Slow down, drop her off, and go home."

I told him I would and went, slowly, on my way. I never saw Officer Suckley again. But thank God for him! He could have easily arrested me, and I would have lost my license and possibly my admission to BU. Who the hell knows what would have happened to me.

Ever since that night, I have thought of my mangled half-finger as a good-luck charm. If I hadn't had that lawnmower accident, I might never have met Officer Suckley. But because of my lucky finger, I was saved.

Nobody wants bad stuff to happen, but let's face it, it does. None of us is perfect. Life is a learning process. So let's get real. Let's come to grips with our mistakes and the bad stuff that happens to us, and embrace it. The sooner you deal with life as it *really* is rather than as you want it to be, the better. People are always coming to me, telling me their sob stories. They think their lives are over. I share my own stories to confirm that it *is* possible not merely to survive, but to do better than you ever thought. Life isn't over when you screw up. It's just beginning.

Restaurant Lessons to Live By

Never quit. Until it's time.

Sometimes it takes a little while to learn from your mistakes. But until you do, the mistakes keep happening.

Restaurants are neighborhood places. Hire local people. And that goes for many other kinds of businesses, too.

Bad things come with silver linings, and everybody has a lucky finger. What's yours?

CHAPTER THIRTEEN

Cover Your Ass-ets

I once knew a guy, Jimmy, who was the best busser in the history of bussers. I mean, this guy was *amazing*. He could do the entire restaurant by himself. His hands flew across the tables as he grabbed plates and glasses and placed them efficiently in his tray. It was a thing of beauty. If there was a Nobel Prize for bussers, he'd win it.

Over the course of fifteen years, I came to rely on Jimmy. I promoted him to jobs with increasing amounts of responsibility. But Jimmy—I've changed his name—had a dirty little secret. He was a sex maniac. The guy was married with kids, but he couldn't keep his hands to himself. He tried to sleep with the servers (and just about everyone else), and he was constantly cracking lewd jokes and making inappropriate comments.

Our managers and I knew nothing about this—until one day, when a female server came forward claiming sexual harassment. And another female server. And another. I was shocked. I didn't know what to do. Nothing like this had ever happened before. It was a potential disaster. We could get sued, not to mention the damage to our reputation.

I dialed up my attorney and trusted advisor, Jim Rudolph. He said I needed to call Lauren Brenner, an experienced human resources professional. She had worked for other area companies and was now a private consultant to clients. She knew how to handle most any workplace issue.

Lauren came to Davio's that same afternoon. She met the servers who had made allegations and determined that they were telling the truth. Following Lauren's advice, I called Jimmy in and fired him immediately. Everybody thought I would find a way to keep him—move him to another restaurant while paying the girls to drop their claims and keep quiet. But I had no intention of doing that. With two daughters of my own, I have no patience for sexual harassment. Plus Davio's reputation matters to me more than any one person. I'd never cheapen the brand by failing to enforce our workplace policies.

It was a sad and unfortunate situation. I don't know what happened to Jimmy. I'm sure he found a job elsewhere, and I hope he got help for his problem. On our end things worked out fine. The servers who had been harassed stayed on with us and felt satisfied with the way we handled the situation, because we had listened carefully to their claims and let them know that we took them seriously. Expertise and professionalism paid off. Our reputation as a nice, upscale place that cared about team members was safe and secure.

Today, whenever there's a potential harassment problem or labor conflict, Lauren steps in. She runs training seminars, helping our staff understand our code of conduct. But she is just one of a couple dozen professionals I use to keep my business going strong. Our crack team of experts includes lawyers, accountants, insurance guys, restaurant and pack-age designers, IT professionals, workplace safety consultants, electricians, and refrigeration pros, among others. If you're going to start a restaurant of your own, or a business with many team members and any level of complexity, you too will need to assemble experts—and fast. Why? Because busi-nesses are train wrecks waiting to happen. Our restaurants do hundreds of financial transactions a day. We have tons of food coming in and going out, and hundreds of team members running around. A million things could go wrong at any time, from a guest slipping and falling, to a fire breaking out in the kitchen, to yes, a staff person letting his wandering eyes get the best of him.

A lot of restaurateurs shrink away from hiring profession-als. They don't want to pay the money, and they tell them-selves, "That bad stuff can't happen to me! It happens to other guys." Guess what? You *are* the other guy! We all are! Every-thing you've built can go up in smoke overnight. If you're in business long enough, trusted team members will sue you. Local authorities will cite you for a violation. The taxman will knock on your door. Your computer systems and phones will go down. And that's assuming you're trying your level best to play by the rules and run a good, clean shop.

As smart as you are, you can't understand everything that could go wrong. The laws about taxation, leases, employment, and so on are complicated. Accounting and design are compli-cated, too. My IT guy, Charlie, speaks a language I don't even understand! And don't get me started on my financial guy, Mike Douvadjian. You need professionals with deep knowl-edge about their chosen field. Not just any professionals, but people familiar with your particular business. Our accountants, lawyers, and designers specialize in restaurants, so they're able to help us anticipate problems before they happen and prevent what problems do occur from ballooning. We wouldn't be where we are with Davio's without professional advice and counsel; it helps us every single day we're open for business. That's why I tell entrepreneurs this at every stage of their careers: The more successful you are, the more you have to lose. You've got ass-ets. Go cover them!

$\smile$

You might wonder why your advisors have to be experts in your chosen field. Can't you just get that same accountant your best friend used for her dry cleaning business? I'll tell you why: because you can get royally screwed. In 1988, when we decided to open a second Davio's in Brookline, I was using as my accountant a guy recommended to me by one of my mentors, Bobby Hillson at Seaside. One of my big pieces of advice is that you choose professionals carefully and get recommendations from people you trust. Even a good recommendation, though, is no guarantee you're getting good counsel. (Remember the recommendation for a contractor I gave to that doctor, whose wife later ran off with the project foreman? Whoo, boy.) Hillson's accountant, a guy I'll call Stuart, had worked on a restaurant account before, but it turned out he didn't know some of the all-important basics of restaurant accounting.

Not knowing this, I called up Stuart and asked his advice about a burning question I had. A lot of my Columbian kitchen staff were already working thirty-five to forty hours a week at our Boston restaurant, and they wanted to work additional hours in Brookline. They all had second jobs, but they preferred to work with Davio's because we treated them well and our locations were more convenient for them. When they came to me asking for more hours, I agreed, since I liked the idea of the same people doing work at both of our restaurants—it would keep product quality consistent. But to keep labor costs low, I didn't want to pay them overtime. Was I allowed to do that? Were the two restaurants separate in the eyes of the law? I was really young at the time, in my late twenties, and I didn't know any of this stuff.

Stuart said the restaurants were separate. "You've set them up as different corporations," he said. "No problem."

My mind now at ease, I let our staff work as much as they wanted in both of our restaurants, paying them the normal hourly rate. A couple of years went by. We opened a third location in Cambridge, and again, just to be sure, I asked Stuart the same question. Did I need to pay overtime to our Boston or Brookline staff who chose to work additional hours in Cambridge? "No," he said. "Separate company. No issue."

Another few years went by. One day in early 1992, a woman came to see me in the administrative office we kept above our Brookline restaurant. "I'm from the Federal Labor Board," she said, "and I'm here to talk to you about your policies and how you pay people."

I invited her to sit down. I had no idea I was doing anything wrong. "What can I do for you?"

"Do you have people who work here for thirty-five hours a week and then go to work in Cambridge?"

"Yes," I said. "But they're set up as separate corporations. So I'm all set."

She shook her head. "No, you're not."

My heart started pounding. "What do you mean, I'm not?"

"Well, you own them all, right? And your workers are doing the same job in each location?"

"Yep."

"Then you have to pay them time and a half."

I couldn't believe this. "My accountant said it's fine."

She shot me a hard look. "You need to find a new accountant."

I didn't know what to say.

"Let me look at your books," she said. She went over to talk to the bookkeeper, who at the time was doing our payroll.

I was freaking out. I never imagined I'd have a problem like this. I'd purposely asked because I was trying to follow the law.

I called Stuart. "Hey, Stu, you know how we have all the guys working two jobs at two different restaurants? Are you sure that's legal?"

"Steve, no problem whatsoever."

"Well, Stu, guess what? I'm looking right now at a federal agent, and she's telling me we're breaking the law. She's telling me I have to pay time and a half. Do you know how much money I'd have to come up with if they went back two or three years and made me pay the difference in wages?"

It turned out that Stuart was dead wrong. I had been responsible for paying time and a half all along. And now I was potentially responsible for paying around $200,000 in back wages for the past three years!

I got my attorney involved. Jim is a really smart guy with a mind for business. A lot of attorneys are great in court, but Jim also understands all facets of running a business—things like payroll, employment law, leasing, construction, and other real estate issues. Jim has handled most of my business and personal legal work since I first met him twenty-eight years ago. Yet he wasn't an expert in labor law, so he had me hire another attorney, Howard Blume. Howard told me I was guilty as sin. "It's not even close. And Steve, this is a law dating back to 1937. It's not a new thing. Whoever told you that you didn't have to pay time and a half was clueless. The only defense that we have is that you're only thirty-one years old and totally ignorant. In other words, you have no defense. We have to hope they go easy on you."

The federal agents held meetings with me and asked all kinds of questions. They interviewed a couple of managers as well as a group of our team members. It turned out I was doing a number of things wrong. Some kitchen managers were receiving a salary when I should have been paying them hourly. (This is a common practice among restaurateurs trying to avoid paying overtime wages. But it turns out that kitchen managers must spend 50 percent of their time hiring, firing, and doing other managerial tasks in order to receive a salary.) We also weren't giving team members the proper amount of break time. Again, in no way was I trying to get around the law; I was so young that I just had no idea about any of this. And here's the point—I didn't have the proper accounting experts to tell me what to do.

This whole situation was a huge disaster. We were a small company then, and I didn't have a lot of extra money. With legal fees and potential fines, I could have been out of business. In the end, once the feds realized I hadn't intentionally been screwing our staff and they saw how willing I was to cooperate, they went easier on me. I didn't face any criminal charges, and we negotiated the amount of back pay I owed to under $100,000—in addition to my legal fees. None of this ever made it into the media. I was lucky, because since then, similar incidents in Boston involving other restaurants *have* been publicized. If that had happened to us, I probably wouldn't have Davio's today.

The checks for back pay that I wrote to our team members amounted to a small windfall for many of them. Some went back to their home countries and bought cows and houses for their families. Overall, though, I don't think the labor laws worked to their advantage. They could no longer work the extra hours since I couldn't afford to pay overtime, so those who needed the extra money had to go find second jobs elsewhere. Because the economy was bad then, they had a hard time of it. Some of them couldn't find second jobs. In the long term they got hurt.

Meanwhile, I had to go to my bank and borrow about $120,000 to cover what I owed. I had hoped that my clueless accountant would have been willing to give me some money toward the legal fees, since it was his bad advice that got me into this situation to begin with. Fat chance. I never spoke to him again after that phone call when the federal agent was sitting in my office. To this day, he has never apologized to me. At my request my attorney went to see him and asked if he had any malpractice insurance that might cover my losses. "Sorry," he said, "I don't have insurance, and there's nothing I can do." I could have sued Stuart, but I didn't need the extra trouble. So I moved on.

$$\sim$$

My tangle with the Feds was a close call. Ever since, I have been a *lot* more careful about labor laws and, in fact, anything having to do with the law. I do everything—*everything*—by the book. And I make sure that the professionals I hire know about restaurants. My main accountant now is Bob Kiley of Restaurant Accounting Services; he knows the ins and outs of tip credits, accounts with vendors, tax withholdings for different team members, tax obligations we have to local government—you name it. He does everything for us, including our payroll and keeping track of all our numbers. I talk to him almost every day to go over our performance. He helps us monitor our costs so we can redo our menu if necessary to maintain a proper cost-to-sales ratio. I also have another accountant, Dave Duchesneau, who vets all my crazy ideas and prepares our corporate and my personal tax returns. Dave is a master at audits—a skill that any restaurateur needs on hand, since they come fast and furious in our business. Dave checks over Bob's work, which makes me feel even more comfortable that we're fulfilling our legal obligations.

As careful and knowledgeable as I am, legal problems *still* arise, and my attorney Jim Rudolph is as indispensible as ever. While I was writing this book, I had to fight a frivolous lawsuit filed by a former team member I'll call Youssef, a dark-skinned man from France. This guy had worked with us for almost fifteen years, starting as a busser and eventually becoming a server. He had a temper, and we'd given him a number of warnings. He was always arguing with someone and often didn't enter his tips correctly into our system, so as to avoid paying taxes. I probably should have fired him, but Youssef had been with us since almost the very beginning, and I cared so much for him. On a number of occasions, I had even loaned him sizable sums of money. The last of these, a loan of $3,000, he has yet to pay back.

I asked Youssef to go to anger management sessions, but he never did. We were finally forced to put him on probation in 2007, when he told a female server to "fuck off." (As you know, we don't tolerate the f-word at Davio's.) She came to me the next day crying, claiming that Youssef was bullying her and that she was afraid he would physically hurt her. Much as I liked Youssef, it was hard to hear her account. I was bullied as a kid, and I remember what that felt like. I couldn't stand the thought of anything that even resembled bullying taking place at Davio's. I sat down with Youssef and told him that this was the last straw and he needed to get psychological help. He would take the week off, and when he came back, he would provide us with proof that he was getting help.

You might wonder why I still was reluctant to fire Youssef outright. In the restaurant business we frequently come across people with substance abuse or other personal problems, and if I can, I want to help them. In many cases these are good people with real talent and skill; they just need someone to believe in them, support them, and give them a chance. We've had many people who are "in the program," as we say. Instead of firing them, we let them get drug counseling, therapy, medical help—whatever they need. Since they're on our subsidized health insurance plan, they're covered. They get to choose their course of treatment, but we have to approve it, and we check in with them every week to make sure that they're actually following through. Sometimes, people do get sober, get off drugs, or work out their personal issues, and it's great to see; Davio's becomes a turning point in their lives. Other times, they still can't turn themselves around, and we have to let them go.

Youssef returned the next week with proof that he had been to an emergency room and that the doctors had told him that he was "not crazy." It was the most bizarre note from a doctor that I'd ever seen. As I explained to him, "I didn't say you were crazy; I said you needed anger management classes." I sent him away again to get help. I invited him to go to his mosque and talk to someone there, if he thought it would be productive. When he came back a week later, he still hadn't gotten any help. "I'll put you on the schedule next week on good faith," I told him, "but you need to give me a letter saying that you're in anger management."

And that was it. I never heard from him again. That is, until 2009, when he filed a discrimination claim against us with the Massachusetts Commission Against Discrimination (MCAD). MCAD is probably the most liberal employee rights organization in the country, yet when it saw our evidence, it threw out Youssef's claim! A couple of years later, we got a letter from a new lawyer Youssef had retained. This letter claimed racial discrimination. According to Youssef, one of our senior managers had called him names and disparaged him in racial terms.

This was utterly ridiculous—an outright lie! We decided to mediate this claim before a retired judge to finally put it to bed. After reviewing the evidence, the judge, not surprisingly, took our side. I don't know for sure, but I suspect he told Youssef that he didn't really have a case, and that Youssef should feel lucky I seemed to have forgotten the $3,000 I loaned him and go on his way. But Youssef evidently wasn't satisfied with this; he insisted on having his day in court. So we wound up trying the case before a jury. I could have settled, but I wasn't about to. I hate liars. No way was I going to reward this one.

I won't bother narrating what happened in the courtroom. Suffice it to say that Youssef didn't have a case. All he had were false allegations. The jury found in our favor. It was really great to go through the case and see the American legal system come to a correct and just verdict. The legal fees cost me more than $75,000 over five years. My insurance didn't cover it, but I didn't care—I was happy to have fought this one. Our team members, too, felt happy. They high-fived me when they heard the news, because they felt like their former colleague had been trying to damage the good name of Davio's, which we all take so seriously.

Have you ever heard of an employer helping out a team member by loaning him thousands of dollars, never getting paid back, not bothering to collect, and then being *sued!?* What is the world coming to? Sometimes, I guess, life just works out like this. You do everything possible to treat people right, everything possible to protect yourself against legal problems, and stuff still happens. The key is to protect yourself. Thanks to the great representation Jim and his team gave me, we've been able to continue serving both our guests and inner guests without missing a beat.

Besides keeping you out of trouble, having real experts on your side can also help you make the most of your business opportunities. First and foremost, you need a great banking relationship. I would never have been able to grow were it not for Scott Dufresne and Tom Young at First Republic Bank. These guys believe in me, so when I come up with a great new business concept, they're ready to back me. Restaurant people come to me all the time and ask, "How do you get so much capital for your new ventures?" Well, Scott and Tom know I'll pay them back, because I have been very careful never to miss a payment in the past. If you're just starting out, I'd advise you to start slowly with small loans that you pay back. Build a strong credit history for your business. And all along, make sure you show a profit and can document it with credible, well-kept books. You'll see that your bank will be very happy to lend you money down the road for bigger and better projects.

Once you have the financing lined up, you also need excellent designers and builder reps on hand to make the most of a new restaurant opportunity. My design specialist, Steve Todisco, is one of the best. He puts great thought into making sure that our layouts and interior decor allow for a high-quality, comfortable guest experience. There is so much that goes into it. Is there a good, natural flow in the place? Do we have enough furniture in the right places? Is the furniture tasteful? How about the art on the walls? Is the kitchen located close enough to the dining room? How will servers move between the kitchen and the dining room? Is there enough room for guests to stand while waiting for a table? And then there are laws we need to follow that only experienced restaurant designers know about. Do we have the required number of bathrooms and fire exits for our guests and inner guests? Are our exits to code? How about the heating and cooling systems?

All of this stuff translates into money, because if guests don't feel comfortable dining in a high-end establishment like ours, they're not coming back. But Steve also contributes to our bottom line in an even more direct way. Back on Newbury Street, we were always trying to think of ways to accommodate more guests in our small space, and we were always bumping up against the limits. Nowadays, maximizing capacity is one of the first things I look at. According to my calculations, each chair I have in a restaurant like ours on Arlington Street brings in $35,000 per year in gross sales. Ten more chairs means an extra $350,000. That's not chump change! I've gone into restaurants that are so poorly designed that they could have put another fifty seats in, but instead, there's empty space or other furniture in the wrong places. That can make the difference between a restaurant's success or failure! But you also never want guests to feel like they're sitting on top of one another; you need to keep to a happy medium, and Steve's knowledge and creativity get us there.

Even if you have a great designer like Steve, you need to complement his or her skill set with that of a top-notch builder rep. Dave Middleton has built hundreds of restaurants around the country, including the Palm and Morton's.

Today, he oversees the building of all our restaurants—everything from hiring the contractors to getting permits and obtaining liquor licenses. Not only does he free me up to focus on the actual running of my existing businesses; he also helps me make sure that Steve's incredible designs are financially viable and executed on budget. Designers are great, but they don't always focus on the money. Hire a designer and no builder rep, and you'll quickly find yourself in the poorhouse! Because Dave understands well all the different cost elements inherent in building a restaurant, he brings Steve's ideas to life without breaking the bank.

I have known for years that a restaurant designer can make all the difference, but I never gave much thought to the people who design boxes for packaged foods you buy in the grocery store. As you might expect, these people can make a *huge* difference, too. When we initially came out with our Davio's spring roll items, we were only selling to stadiums, convention centers, hotels, and restaurants, so we had a plain white box. Then in 2009, when we wanted to go into retail outlets, we hired a designer to create a real box for us. I hate to say it, but it looked horrible. It had very little connection to Davio's brand, our history, what we were all about, and it didn't feel right. At the time, of course, I thought it was great—but what did I know? Except to grab some ice cream, I hardly ever went to the frozen food section for prepared foods; as a foodie, I'm all about fresh. I was focused on sales, and we did get some small orders from places like Roche Bros. and Stop & Shop, so I didn't give the design a second thought.

In 2010 I was at a party and happened to meet two designers, Bill and Dan, from a company called Motiv. Bill offered to come by Davio's and look at our packaging, so I said sure. He called me up the next day. "Steve, look, you're a great guy, and your reputation is great. I love you, but I gotta tell you, that box you have is disgusting. You should be embarrassed by it; in fact, you should go to the stores and just buy up all the products with the box and throw them out!"

It was hard news to take at first, but I listened. I wound up working with a couple of Bill's colleagues to totally redesign the box. It cost me tens of thousands of dollars, but their work was brilliant. They went to Shaw's and photographed the entire frozen foods section, so that I had a frame of reference. They studied our brand, visiting our restaurant and taking pictures. Most frozen food boxes are red, but noticing that our interior decor uses a lot of purple, they designed a purple-themed box. They put my picture on it, because they figured if I'm going to be selling the product in new markets around the country, consumers needed to know a real person is behind it. They needed to know who I was, how we got started, and what we were about. We put stories on the box, too, such as how we came up with the various flavors of spring rolls we sell. (I'd tell you the chicken parm one, which involves Wayne Leabeaux, Bruce Springsteen's assistant, and a real chicken parm guy, but maybe you should just go to your local grocery store and buy a box!)

Here's our old box. See how dull and lifeless it is?

And now, here's our new box. What a difference, right?

If I had any doubts whether the box redesign was a smart investment, they were dismissed in one day, when Stephanie from Yankee Trader and I went down to Atlanta to sell spring rolls in the new box to Costco. We'd been there the year before, and they had declined to make a purchase. This time, I pulled out the boxes, put them on a table, and walked away with a $500,000 sale! "Wow," they said, "you guys really stepped it up with these spring rolls!"

"Well, it's the same product as last year."

"Yeah, but your box was embarrassing. We didn't want to say anything, but we just couldn't put that product in our stores with that box."

So there you go. Costco today has grown its account with us and is now one of our biggest customers. All because we got the right designers in to design a better box.

I don't care what it costs (and don't tell Motiv I'm saying this)—if you're going to come out with a serious packaged food product, you can't just do it yourself. You have to get people who have dedicated their careers to designing boxes. Otherwise, you're just spinning your wheels.

Oh, one more thing. I was so ashamed about our old boxes—and so convinced how much the new boxes mattered—that whenever I saw our old boxes in a store, I would buy them all up, and yes, throw them out!

⌐⌐

I hope by now you're seeing the value of good professional help. Yet once you have good professionals on your team, people you've vetted and whose work you know you can rely on, you still can't just sit back and forget about them. You have to watch them and demand that they keep their own services up to date and high quality.

Let me end this chapter by telling you about Gary, my insurance guy. He was with me for twenty-five years. He wasn't just my insurance guy; he was a good friend. We had been through hell together. Back in 1991, we had a fire at our Newbury Street location. I lived five blocks from the restaurant, and one day when I was at home, I heard fire trucks. A moment later, my phone rang. It was bad—a kitchen fire that had gotten in the flue and spread. Nobody was at fault—it was just one of those things—but $500,000 of damage resulted. I've said that bad news often turns out to have a silver lining, and this is another great example. When we used the insurance money to renovate, we were able to expand, adding more stoves and a better exhaust system to the kitchen. I even wound up taking over space next door used by a hair salon and adding sixty more seats.

I had general liability insurance, so I was covered for the fire damage, but I didn't have business interruption insurance. That meant I had no money to pay the staff, the rent, or our vendors while our restaurant was being repaired. Interruption insurance is *so critical* for any business to have. Back in the day, Gary really came through for me. He had his company loan me $10,000 to help with my business interruption—not because he had to, but because he wanted to.

As the years passed, Gary continued to help and support me, becoming a close family friend. When I was honored by the Anti-Defamation League at a dinner, he bought a number of seats. I repaid Gary's friendship with loyalty of my own. I kept my insurance business with him for years, even after he moved to a new company. He did our liquor liability insurance and wrote policies for our cars, my houses—everything. I would get called all the time by people who wanted to bid on my insurance needs, and I would always tell them, "Gary is my guy!" I wouldn't even want to meet with them.

One day, Paul Flynn, a guest of ours who eats with us almost every day and who is also in the insurance business, approached me. "You know, Steve, I'd love for my company to have a shot at looking at your insurance portfolio."

"Paul, I'd like to let you, but I've had this guy for twenty-five years."

"But Steve," he said, "I eat here every day. You and I know so many people in common."

I thought about it. My insurance policies were coming up for renewal soon. What would it hurt to let this company take a look? Gary was a real pro; he was probably getting me the best possible deal. This other company would come in around the same price as I was already paying, in which case I'd just tell them no. "Okay," I said to Paul. "Send someone in and I'll have him look at everything. But no promises."

Steve Richards, one of Paul's partners, came in, and I insisted that he give me prices for the exact same coverage I was already receiving. I wanted to compare policies apples to apples. He went away and did his analysis. He had a great idea: Liberty Mutual happened to be my landlord on Arlington Street, so why not get quotes from them? This is something that Gary hadn't done. When Steve came back, he had surprising news: It turned out he could save me $50,000 a year. For the exact same coverage. In fact, it wasn't the exact same coverage. It was a little *better* coverage.

I had been working with Gary for so long that I wasn't about to let him go without giving him a chance. I called him up. "Gary, we have a problem. Can you cut $50,000 off my insurance costs?" Turned out he couldn't. I wound up changing agents. It really hurt me to have to do it, but we're talking about a substantial amount of money!

My wife, Pam, knew Gary, and she also knew the esteem I held him in. The night I switched over to Steve Richards, Pam and I were driving somewhere together. I leaned over. "You'll never guess what I did today."

"What?"

"I fired Gary."

"You did *not*."

"I did."

It tore me up to tell her. Even as I write this, I find myself getting emotional. I pride myself on being loyal to people who have helped me. It's just something I do. I've got vendors I've bought from since Davio's first went into business. Accardi Foods. Boston Showcase. M.S. Walker. Paul Marks. Martignetti Companies. But as always, my ultimate loyalty goes to my company and to the Davio's brand. Hundreds of team members are counting on me. I would be letting them down if I allowed my personal relationships get in the way of sound business decisions. So sadly, the decision to fire Gary was a no-brainer.

I'll say it again: You have to have qualified experts by your side, protecting your interests. But nobody is perfect, and the interests at stake are yours. Keep your eyes open. Ask tough questions. Explore your options. Make changes when you have to.

The responsibility for covering your ass-ets ultimately lies with *you*.

Restaurant Lessons to Live By

Sometimes bussers make messes of their own. Make sure you've got someone on hand who can clean it all up.

Choose professionals wisely. Get recommendations from friends. Even then, pay attention. You don't want the Feds knocking at your door.

Not all professionals know the intricacies of your industry. Choose lawyers, accountants, and others who do.

You can do everything right, take every precaution—and still get sued. Make sure you've got a heavy hitter like Jim Rudolph by your side, and you'll be fine.

The right professionals don't just protect your existing assets. They help you build new ones. Hire a better graphic designer, get a better box.

When it comes to covering your ass-ets, the buck stops with you!

CHAPTER FOURTEEN

Protect Your Rep

There's a friend of mine—I'll call him Mitch—who owned a restaurant in Boston but lived out of state with his wife and kids. He stayed in Boston during the week and went home on the weekends. One weekday night, he got into an argument with a woman who was supposedly his girlfriend. This woman called the police, and Mitch got arrested for allegedly beating her up. The next day, Mitch's mug shot appeared in a Boston newspaper.

After the story broke Mitch had to focus on saving his marriage. He spent more time at home and barely came in to manage his restaurant. Predictably, it went downhill. Who wants to go to a restaurant owned by a guy who allegedly cheated on his wife and beat up women? I know I didn't—and this guy was my friend! Eating in his restaurant would have made me feel like I was supporting or condoning his bad behavior. A lot of other people agreed with me. Soon after Mitch's scandal broke, business dropped off and he started having money problems. Within a year he had sold his business and left town. I haven't seen him since.

Reputation is everything. In restaurants or any business, we all care not merely about the quality we're getting, or the value for the money, or the purchase experience—we care about the *people* we're doing business with. This means you can't do anything stupid. It was true thirty years ago when I first started, and it's even truer today, given how fast word spreads on social media. As I've said in this book, being a restaurateur is about serving others and exceeding expectations. It's *all* about the guest. When you screw up like Mitch did, you're not serving guests—you're just pushing them away!

Stupid behavior chips away at your business. One day, you're the hottest ticket in town. You have the best food. People love you. Then you screw up and the week after, ten guests don't come. The week after that, twelve don't. A month later, fifteen. Before you know it, you're nothing.

Any business is replaceable. Even yours, my friend. So be good, and protect your rep!

~

Most restaurateurs I know are not as clueless as Mitch. They care about their brand and are aware that poor judgment can destroy what they've built. Although they tend to be egotistical, most are nice people who treat others with dignity and respect. Yet restaurateurs don't always realize as fully as they might how fragile their establishment's reputation is. The scary thing is that it isn't only your behavior or what you say that can prove damaging—it's how your staff and guests conduct themselves, too.

You obviously can't control what other people say or do. Still, you can take steps to protect yourself. First of all, collect a lot of pocket favors. Why? Because if catastrophe strikes and a scandal does break out, individuals are a lot more willing to forgive you and your company if you've done good deeds for them in the past. Likewise, an entire community will give you the benefit of the doubt if you've consistently, over years, given back. (Remember the old Jimmy Stewart movie *It's a Wonderful Life*?) These days, not a week goes by when I'm not doing one or two fund-raising events for local charities. I do cooking demonstrations, make cash donations, and support the charitable endeavors of other restaurateurs. I do it because I care, because I love the community, but I also realize that if I help others, they'll help in my moment of need, if I ever have one. You don't wait until July to find a guy to fix your air-conditioning, do you? Not a good idea. So why wait until you have a problem before you start getting people on your side? Establish those relationships right now.

A related point: Don't wait until you have a problem to hire a PR company. Get one *now*. In the old days you had time to respond, because most people got their news from newspapers, and newspapers came out only once a day. These days, the formal news cycle is gone. Seconds matter. If you're not ready to respond to an allegation or a rumor about you, you're leaving yourself vulnerable. In the heat of a scandal, you don't have time to interview a PR company. I know that if anything bad ever happened to me or our restaurants, I would have my own in-house PR person, Anny, on the phone immediately. If necessary, we would also bring in George Regan, the head of my Boston PR company. He would be ready to go to bat for us, no matter where in the world he happened to be. We would handle the problem as best as we possibly could—and hopefully put a quick end to it.

I'm getting ahead of myself. It's better to find ways of *preventing* your staff from causing scandals in the first place. We have a policy at Davio's that all media contact goes through me. Reporters are always looking for a story, so you have to be careful what you say. If we have some kind of problem in Philadelphia or Atlanta, my general managers might talk to the press, but they always run it by me first. We have a pretty tight social media policy, so as to prevent team members from saying something, either accidentally or on purpose, that reflects poorly on us. And of course we have a full-time team member who looks at Facebook, Twitter, Yelp, and the like every day for anything bad that anyone might be saying about us.

Another thing we do is take a lot of care to hire the very best people. We ask around to find out about the reputations of people who want to work with us. They may be skilled at their jobs, but how are they as people? Sometimes we think we love a person and are ready to hire her, only to learn that she has a drug problem or is hard to get along with. I also always make sure to ask people during interviews what they do for charity. If I come across a twenty-two-year-old server, bartender, or cook who donates his time to a local church or mosque, or who has volunteered with his family at a food bank on Thanksgiving since childhood, I can be pretty sure that he's both oriented toward serving others well and just a good, kind, considerate person in general.

Of course, some people manage to fool you. When this happens, you have to be really good about getting rid of them as quickly as possible. One year, I had a real shock when I found out a team member we'd hired was a die-hard racist. I was on my way to a meeting of the Anti-Defamation League, of which I'm a strong supporter, when I ran into a couple of our servers. They asked where I was headed, and I told them. "What's the Anti-Defamation League?" they asked. "Well," I said, "it's an organization that fights racism, bullying, and anti-Semitism. It started out being a Jewish organization, but it's gotten to be much more."

The servers shot each other funny looks.

"What?" I asked.

"Are you going to talk to Nick?" one of them asked.

I told them I didn't know what they were talking about.

"Well, just the other day there was an African-American party of six that sat down in his station. He said something really bad."

I asked them to repeat what he had said—and it was a totally unacceptable racial dig. I freaked out. I was *livid*. I couldn't believe that one of our team members had been so disrespectable. Nick (I've changed the names of people in this story) was a skilled server who had previously worked at other top restaurants, but I didn't care. We had to do something about this.

I raced over to another team member, Harry, who had worked some shifts with Nick. "Hey, tell me about Nick. Is he okay? What's going on with him?"

Harry confirmed Nick's remarks. Fortunately, the guests hadn't heard.

I couldn't believe it. "Harry, stuff like this happens, and you don't tell me about it?"

I asked around some more and discovered that Nick was making anti-Semitic comments, too. It was outrageous. I'm not just an Anti-Defamation League board member; I'm vice chair of its Board of Overseers! I don't want my people making slurs about *anyone*. It goes against everything I believe in. And talk about bad for business. We have guests of many ethnicities—African American, Jewish, Hispanic, Asian—and we love them all. As an employer, we're the United Nations of restaurants; our team members come from over thirty different countries (I know because I've counted). If guests had overheard Nick's racist statements in the restaurant, it could have been a disaster for us. Our reputation in the local area would have been ruined.

It just goes to show that even the most careful interview process sometimes fails. And it underlines how important it is for the owner or general manager to be present as much as possible, to catch mistakes that fall through the cracks. Our other team members were not racists by any means, but each had overheard a small snippet of what Nick had said. They didn't think guests had been affected, so they were hesitant to speak up to management. That was the second thing I had to work on. But first I called Joe, our general manager, who hadn't yet heard about the racist slur, and told him I wanted Nick out.

He was gone that day.

⌒

Now you understand why a guy like me has trouble sleeping at night! Sometimes, it seems like a PR disaster is looming around every corner. Nobody, including you, has to actually do or say anything bad to screw up your reputation. Just the *suggestion* of misdeeds is enough to keep guests away, sink morale among inner guests, and disrupt your business.

For this reason I want to qualify a point I made earlier in the book. In chapter five I argued that business owners need to treat team members with dignity and respect, helping them out when they're sick and even going so far as to avoid a generic, soulless term like *employee.* But I do think it's possible to be *too* nice and tolerate behavior you shouldn't. When you do this, you not only risk weakening the guest experience. You put your restaurant's reputation at stake, and with it, your very survival.

We once had a sommelier at Arlington Street, Frank, who was a bit of a prima donna with our other team members but great with the guests. He could recommend exactly the right pairing for your entrées, and at a price point that didn't bankrupt you. He was also a real character, a bit of a local celebrity, and guests loved joking around with him. He always wore loud ties and eccentric suits. I love it when our team members let their personalities shine. You come to Davio's and it's like a box of chocolates—you never know what you'll get, in a good way.

Oh, did I mention that Frank was a big gambler? He even had a column in a large newspaper that offered betting advice. Frank's gambling didn't seem to be affecting his work, so I didn't say anything to him about it. I certainly should have. In 2008 the first signs of trouble emerged. Frank had bet too heavily on March Madness and called me up, terribly upset. "Steve, I need to talk to you. I need to borrow $15,000 and I need it today, or I'm going to get beat up. This is serious!"

What did I do?

I gave him the $15,000, and we worked out a plan for him to pay me back. I think it was $500 a month initially. He only paid $5,000 of the $15,000. To this day, he still owes me the rest.

That was nothing compared to the damage he almost caused me a year later. One morning, I opened up the *Boston Globe* to a headline that read something like, "Order Your Wine and Place Your Bet at Davio's."

I almost had a heart attack.

It turned out that Frank had gotten indicted for gambling. A month or two before, he was caught on tape taking bets from a known mafia figure. And get this: He was allegedly taking bets *in the Davio's wine room.*

An hour later, Jim Rudolph called me. "Steve, have you seen the *Globe*?"

I indicated that I had.

"Well, what are you going to do about it?"

"I'm going to talk to Frank today."

Jim was stunned. "What do you mean you're going to talk to him? You have to fire him! You have to get him out of your place. *Right now.*"

"But this guy owes me ten grand."

"I don't care what he owes you. Do you want to lose your business?"

I hadn't thought about it, but because I hold a liquor license, I have to fill out a form every year that says that I have not committed a felony. I can't even be around people who are criminals, so the fact that I now had a team member charged with committing a serious crime on our premises—and with a mobster, no less—could get me in serious trouble. Not to mention what our guests might think about me and our restaurant. Frank's little gambling problem had become our problem. It was threatening the Davio's brand.

Oh. My. God! I called Frank in and fired him right then and there.

When I think back about why I hadn't fired him much earlier, I realize it wasn't just the fact that he was good with the guests—it's because I also feel a deep urge to stand by troubled team members. During the early years I used to fire people right and left. Then I discovered that we could actually save people, helping them break their self-destructive habits. That felt so good that I wanted to do it again and again, and the urge still hasn't left me. I've also seen people totally self-destruct, which had a huge impact on me.

One of my original chefs, Scotty, left in the early '90s to open his own restaurant. He was an alcoholic and drug abuser, and his abuse cost him one of his kidneys. One day in 1997, he came to see me. "Steve, I want to come back to work for you." I made him agree to join Alcoholics Anonymous and get therapy. We assigned him to Davio's in Cambridge. Then one July 4, the busiest day of the year in that location, he didn't show up for work. I knew immediately that something was wrong. I sent fellow chef Rodney down to Scotty's house in a Boston suburb to get him. Rodney called and told me that Scotty was home, but he was really drunk and depressed. "He doesn't want to talk to you, Steve. He's really upset with himself." I jumped into my car and went to Scotty's house anyway, but Rodney was right, he wouldn't see me. Two weeks later, Scotty was dead. His remaining kidney couldn't take the extreme alcohol poisoning.

When you live through something like that, trust me, you do whatever you can to help people. And I think part of me thought I could help Frank get past his gambling addiction.

I didn't lose my business or my reputation over Frank's arrest. The whole thing blew over. I'm not even sure Frank went to jail. Ever since, I have been far more careful not to tolerate bad behavior. If you're a team member of ours and you have a problem, I'll work with you up to a point. I'll keep you on the program. But when you go too far, if you avoid the warnings we give, I won't hesitate to let you go. I have no patience. The Davio's brand and our reputation are too important, and too fragile. Again, our brand is bigger than any individual. When you mess with the brand, you have to leave.

I should add that firing isn't always an easy solution to reputational challenges. Sometimes you have to go further and even swallow your pride and sense of what's right. Carol was a baker at our Cambridge restaurant who didn't get along well with the rest of the team. If somebody went into the dessert station and took something or didn't replace it, she didn't go to the managers but instead wrote notes around the kitchen like, "Don't take things!" and "Your mother doesn't work here!" Just signs everywhere, which others found really rude. We warned her, but she kept up with the notes. Realizing that everybody hated her, we decided to let her go.

What happened? She sued us for discrimination. Previously, Carol had developed carpal tunnel syndrome that required an operation, so she claimed that we had fired her because of her disability. Simply not true! She wanted a big chunk of money from us, and I wouldn't have it. We prepared for a jury trial.

Before the trial started the judge called us into his chambers with Jim Rudolph and Carol's attorney. The judge told me that if the case went to trial, I would probably lose, since many of the jurors came from humble circumstances and would hold a bias against me, the "rich restaurant guy." Even more ominous, if the case became widely publicized, people in the community might jump to conclusions and think that Davio's had no compassion for the rights of workers or for people with disabilities. It didn't matter what had actually happened; if I was smart, I would settle. So I did—to the tune of $20,000.

I *hated* doing that. I knew beyond a shadow of a doubt what had really happened, and that we didn't owe Carol a dime. We were the ones getting screwed here, not her. But for the sake of maintaining our reputation, I paid the extra money. Businesses and their brands require goodwill. Squander that, and you've squandered everything.

At the beginning of this book, I talked about my experiences growing up in a big immigrant family. I learned so much from my relatives—thoughts of them inform everything I do. In general, I think the connection between family and restaurants runs deep. Many restaurants are quite literally family businesses. Even in those that are not, staff tends to think of themselves as family (assuming the restaurant is well run). And, of course, restaurants must do everything they can to welcome guests in, treating them with the warmth and kindness they would show their own relatives.

I first learned to protect my rep from my dad. As an Italian American, he was so proud of the DiFillippo family. He wanted our name to be a *great* name that was respected by the community, and he told us kids from an early age that it was our job to help make it so. "The DiFillippo name," he used to say, "don't ever, *ever* mess it up!" It was my responsibility to be a nice person, work hard, make a good living, and give back to the less fortunate. From the very beginning of Davio's, I always tried to do the right thing and maintain my reputation because I didn't want to disappoint my dad. That's why I worked so hard when I first bought Davio's to get rid of all the druggies and alcoholics that had been working there. I was terrified that someone would overdose in the bathroom, that we'd be in the news, and that my reputation would be ruined. I've found over the last thirty years that it's not that hard, really, to keep a good name. Just do the right thing and take reasonable precautions, and you should be fine.

I got the message, but not all of my peers did. Remember my mentor growing up, Mr. Sampsonas? He was a pretty serious dude in the restaurant industry. Back in the day, he invented the idea of surf and turf—pairing steak with seafood. That's right, he dreamed that up. His restaurant, the Continental, was wildly successful, and during the early '80s, when Mr. Sampsonas was in his late sixties, his older son began to take it over. Unfortunately, this son got into dealing cocaine and went to prison for ten years. With nobody to take over the business, Mr. Sampsonas wound up selling it. He was never the same after that. What happened to his son and his business just broke his heart. To make matters worse, his younger son also got into drugs, became an addict, and lost everything. (Thank God he also had two daughters, who turned out great!)

These days, I ask Pam and my kids to be just as aware of the DiFillippo family name as my father asked me to be. I've seen prominent restaurateurs get their names in the paper because family members got involved in drugs or legal problems. It's not good for the business or for the brand. I've also seen prominent families who are disciplined about protecting the family name, keeping any disagreements private and working hard in public to support and help one another. I have to say, Pam is amazing. Even if we disagree about something on a given day, she always puts on a good face. My kids are learning, too, and when they slip, I'm right there to show them the way.

My oldest son, Michael, has shown interest in the business, and he has already spent some time working as a prep cook, busser, food runner, host, and server at Davio's. This past summer, we had a little incident that told me he still has some growing up to do. We have a beach house about fifteen minutes away from our main home, and we usually spend the entire summer on the water. One day, Pam and I were out with two of our four kids and decided to stop at our main house. We were in two cars, and Pam arrived about ten minutes before I did. When I come through the front door, my thirteen-year-old daughter Ella came running up to me. "Dad, Dad, Dad, Michael's in there, in the living room!"

"Oh, great," I said, not paying much attention.

"He's with a girl!"

"Really?" I asked, my interest piqued.

"And they're drinking and I think she works at Davio's."

Whoa. What?! I went to the living room to find Michael on the couch drinking beer and watching TV with a beautiful twenty-year-old Swedish girl named Emma. She worked as a hostess at Davio's.

I was furious. "Michael," I said, gesturing for his attention. "Can I talk to you?"

We went into the kitchen, out of earshot. Then I went ballistic on him. "What are you doing? Are you crazy? There are, like, twenty things wrong with what you're doing." He didn't seem to understand, so I went on. "First, what are you doing serving beer? She's underage. And you take her to our *house?* You can't bring someone from the restaurant to our house." I try to keep my personal and business life separate as much as possible—something I had talked to him about many times. The ironic thing is that he was to move into his own apartment two days later. Couldn't he wait two days?

"But Dad," he protested, "why aren't you at the beach?"

I wanted to kill him. "Excuse me? Why am I *at my own house?*"

He shrugged. "I don't see what the big deal is."

"The big deal? You don't know what kind of trouble you can get into doing this. She could claim harassment—are you crazy?" I was truly baffled. "To you, I'm the golden goose. You don't mess with the golden goose. You *protect* the golden goose." His car keys were lying on the counter, so I handed them to him. "Look, I want you outta here right now. You drive her home. I don't want her driving after she's been drinking."

He took the keys unhappily.

"This is not how we are in this family," I said as he walked away. "We don't use what we have to impress girls, or anybody else for that matter. What were you thinking?"

At the kitchen entrance he turned to me with a little smirk on his face. "Dad, can you just give us twenty minutes?"

I scowled at him and waved him off. "Fine. Twenty minutes."

I huffed upstairs and into my bedroom, where Pam was. I'm embarrassed to admit it now, but I made sure I closed the door before I broke out laughing.

"What's so funny?" Pam asked.

I told her that Michael had asked me for twenty more minutes. It was a guy thing. I just thought that was so hilarious. I remember what it was like being his age and obsessed with girls.

"It's not funny," Pam said. "I don't know why you're laughing."

I stopped, realizing that as usual, Pam was right. This *was* serious business, and I needed to treat it as such. Michael didn't understand the importance of maintaining our reputation—not just for the sake of our family, but for the sake of Davio's. He thought he could use his leverage as my son to show off and get girls. No way!

In the months that followed, Michael graduated from Boston University in the School of Hospitality Administration. He and I agreed that he would stop working at Davio's and get an outside job with a top hotel chain. If he wanted to learn the business, he'd have to spend at least a few years starting at the bottom and making his own way. I think that every business owner with kids should have them go off and prove themselves before coming back to work with the family. I know that Jonathan Kraft, for example, worked for Bain and Company before going back to work with his dad, Robert. In my case, I wanted Michael to develop the humility that comes with working late nights and weekends, busting his butt to impress his managers and please guests. If he could prove to me that he could survive, and that he understood what running a restaurant was really about—serving others, not stoking your ego—then he'd be ready to build a career at Davio's. He had to be ready to devote himself to building Davio's reputation, not just having a good time as the boss's son. He had to have a real passion for this business.

So far, the signs are good. He got a job at the Ritz working the front desk. He has been putting in long hours, sometimes sleeping as little as three or four hours a night. He recently got promoted to manager of the hotel restaurant—an accomplishment that made me very proud, since it entirely reflected his own efforts (good thing Emma the beautiful Swede doesn't work there). When his general manager, knowing who I am, asked him why he was working there, Michael said, "Well, I need to develop my own reputation in this business, not my father's." I was proud again when I heard that. It seems like he's starting to get it. Hopefully, I will be as successful in transmitting values and a respect for what our family has built as my dad was with me.

Davio's is so important. The people. The brand. The food. I just care about it so much. I believe in what we do and the role we play in the community. I want to grow Davio's, so that we can please more and more guests, employ more and more people, and do more and more good in the world. I want Davio's to outlive me, and I dream that people everywhere will look at Davio's wherever they encounter our brand and say, "Hey, those guys aren't just good—they're great! They exceeded my expectations."

I will continue to work my hardest to earn this great reputation. My hope is that you will likewise take pleasure in building a business, brand, and reputation of your own. Be strong. Work hard. Do plenty of pocket favors. Pay attention to the other pieces of restaurant wisdom in this book. And please, take time out to celebrate, using the recipes in this book to enjoy life a little. One day, if you're lucky, I hope you'll sit in your busy restaurant, surrounded by guests, and marvel at just how far you've come. And if you're like me, you'll then go happily back to work, reminding yourself once again: *It's all about the guest.*

Restaurant Lessons to Live By

You can't build a strong, stable business if you don't behave.

Reputations are fragile. Protect yourself by doing tons *of pocket favors. Get a PR firm. And select carefully the people you bring on board.*

A racist—at Davio's? I don't think so! Sometimes your best efforts to weed out bad team members can come up short. You have to stay vigilant.

It's not just what you do that matters. It's how people per-ceive *what you do. Go the extra mile and guard against even the appearance of bad behavior.*

Reputation is a family affair. My son thought he didn't have to think about protecting our name and the Davio's brand. Boy, was he wrong.

Acknowledgments

This book came into being thanks to the talent and hard work of many people. Joan Wilder helped create the initial proposals, spending hours with me taping stories and then working to bring some order to it. Lorin Rees of the Rees Literary Agency liked what he saw and became my agent. Thanks so much, Lorin, for seeing the potential and helping us refine the book concept.

From the moment I spoke with Mary Norris at Lyons Press, I knew I wanted to publish with her. She understood the book and has been amazing with her advice and guidance. As an added bonus, we closed the deal at Pepe's Pizzeria in New Haven, Connecticut, one of my all-time favorites.

Seth Schulman of the Providence Word and Thought Company and his beautiful colleague Chrissy helped me write the manuscript. We met for weeks over lunch at Davio's in Foxboro, working our way through my stories and our menu, and sharing a lot of laughs in the process. Thank you, Seth, for getting words on the page so quickly and effortlessly. Thank you, too, to Herb Chambers, Jim Rudolph, Anny Deirmenjian, and my sister Donna DiFillippo for their thoughtful review of the manuscript. Your sharp comments have made this a much better book.

I owe a huge debt to my mom and dad for always inspiring me to be the very best I could be. Also to the rest of the DiFillippo family for their ongoing support, and to my extended family, the many exceptional team members who have worked with us these past thirty years. Without all of you, there wouldn't be a Davio's today.

My greatest thanks go to my wife, Pam, and my kids, Katherine, Michael, Ella, and Max. I know that living with me is not all peaches and cream. You have sacrificed so much so that I could realize my dreams and help build Davio's into what it is today.

Thank you, finally, to all the readers of this book. Exceeding expectations is not rocket science. It takes hard work and more hard work. I hope you'll get up every day, do your best, and most of all, have a great time doing it. Please stop in to one of our restaurants and say hi. We'd love to welcome you into the Davio's family. And if you happen to think of a delicious new flavor for our spring rolls, just let us know!

About the Author

After graduating from Boston University in 1982, Steve DiFillippo, CEO of Davio's Northern Italian Steakhouse, attended the Cambridge School of Culinary Arts. During college and culinary school, he learned the restaurant business from the ground up, working at the three-hundred-seat Seaside restaurant in Boston's Faneuil Hall; he began as a coffee clerk and ended up as executive  chef. In 1985, at the age of twenty-four, after seven years of working full-time in the business, DiFillippo purchased an existing spot named Davio's and completely revamped its menu. The new Davio's was hailed as a renaissance on Boston's Newbury Street and garnered rave reviews for being "innovative, creative, and bold." Over the years, DiFillippo opened more Davio's locations in the Boston area as well as in Philadelphia (1999), Gillette Stadium (2008), and Atlanta (2010), with New York City scheduled for 2013.

In the fall of 2007 DiFillippo launched Davio's popular Philly Cheese Steak Spring Rolls as a retail product. This has evolved into a $10 million retail food business. An expanding line of Davio's products is sold in three thousand markets across forty states, including Costco, BJs, Big Y, and other supermarkets.

DiFillippo is actively involved in numerous civic, professional, and philanthropic organizations and events, including the Rodman Ride for Kids, Raising a Reader MA, and the Cambridge School of Culinary Arts. He was inducted into the Massachusetts Restaurant Association's Hall of Fame in 2008, and the Anti-Defamation League of New England honored him with its Torch of Liberty award in 2010. DiFillippo lives in Wenham, MA, with his wife, Pamela, and their four children.